Praise for *The Illustrated Mark Twain and the* Buffalo Express

"Another welcome edition by Thomas J. Reigstad adds to our appreciation of Mark Twain's early days in Buffalo. Each piece in this collection—combined with images drawn by cartoonists and illustrators across many decades (and one by Mark Twain himself)—elicits chuckles. Twain's comments on Niagara Falls, fake news, cemeteries, war, and taxes still sting smartly today. Reigstad's efforts to gather and comment on Twain's Buffalo pieces—paired with the work of fine cartoonists and illustrators—makes for an enjoyable, illuminating read."—**Barbara Snedecor**, former director of the Center for Mark Twain Studies at Elmira College and author of *Gravity—Selected Letters of Olivia Langdon Clemens*

"Mark Twain's hectic years in Buffalo receive insufficient credit for their impact on his life and writings. Now the foremost expert on this period of Twain's biography, Thomas J. Reigstad, provides deserved focus on his clever *Buffalo Express* writings and the gifted artists who have ingeniously illustrated those writings." —**Alan Gribben**, author of *Mark Twain's Literary Resources*

"Reigstad's book offers invaluable insight into a pivotal period of Mark Twain's early career. His recovery of the writer's previously unknown collaboration with *Express* staff artist John Harrison Mills is a revelation—literary detective work at its best. The volume's inclusion of later illustrations by Tom Toles, Bill Watterson, and Adam Zyglis is simply the delectable icing on top."—**Kerry Driscoll**, author of *Mark Twain among the Indians and Other Indigenous Peoples*

"Mark Twain said he was gratified to be ignorant of art because those who understand it 'find nothing in pictures but blemishes.' He should have lived to see this volume. Reigstad gives us ten Twain stories from his time at the *Buffalo Express* complete with illustrations from Buffalo artists Adam Zyglis, Tom Toles, and Twain himself. And there's not a blemish to be found."—**Erik Brady**, *Buffalo News* contributing columnist

"Reigstad's *The Illustrated Mark Twain and the* Buffalo Express is a wonderful cornucopia of stories written by Twain in his tumultuous years as a new husband, father, homeowner, and editor of a daily newspaper. Presented in their context—with illustrations by gifted artists over the decades—these creations are a swag bag of treasures for readers old and new."—**Darryl Brock**, author of *If I Never Get Back*

"Reigstad is the preeminent authority on Mark Twain's literary career at the *Buffalo Express*. Reigstad's selection of Twain's feature stories in this collection are accompanied by introductions and illustrations that place them in historical context and underscore the humor and satire that are often lost on modern readers." —**Barbara Schmidt**, publisher of twainquotes.com

THE ILLUSTRATED
MARK TWAIN
AND THE
Buffalo Express

10 Stories and over a Century of Sketches

THOMAS J. REIGSTAD

FOREWORD BY LAURA SKANDERA TROMBLEY

NC BOOKS

North Country

An imprint of Globe Pequot, the trade division of The Rowman & Littlefield Publishing Group, Inc.

4501 Forbes Blvd., Ste. 200

Lanham, MD 20706

www.rowman.com

Distributed by NATIONAL BOOK NETWORK

British Library Cataloguing in Publication Information available

Library of Congress Cataloging-in-Publication Data

Names: Twain, Mark, 1835–1910, author. | Reigstad, Thomas J., editor, writer of introduction, writer of added commentary. | Skandera-Trombley, Laura E., writer of foreword.

Title: The illustrated Mark Twain and the Buffalo Express : 10 stories and over a century of sketches / Thomas J. Reigstad ; foreword by Laura Skandera Trombley.

Other titles: Buffalo express.

Description: Essex, Connecticut : North Country Books, [2024] | Includes bibliographical references. | Summary: "Twain's Buffalo Express stories from 1869 and 1870 stand the test of time. But their entertainment value is vastly increased when coupled with visual interpretations provided by talented illustrators (including Twain himself) of yesterday and today"—Provided by publisher.

Identifiers: LCCN 2023021507 (print) | LCCN 2023021508 (ebook) | ISBN 9781493076031 (cloth) | ISBN 9781493076048 (epub)

Subjects: LCSH: Editorials—New York (State)—Buffalo. | Editorial cartoons—New York (State)—Buffalo. | Humorous stories, American—New York (State)—Buffalo. | Buffalo (N.Y.)—History. | United States—History—1865–1898.

Classification: LCC PS1303 .R45 2024 (print) | LCC PS1303 (ebook) | DDC 813/.4—dc23/eng/20230720

LC record available at https://lccn.loc.gov/2023021507

LC ebook record available at https://lccn.loc.gov/2023021508

∞™ The paper used in this publication meets the minimum requirements of American National Standard for Information Sciences—Permanence of Paper for Printed Library Materials, ANSI/NISO Z39.48-1992.

For N. B.

CONTENTS

FOREWORD

"Night before last I had a singular dream." This sentence begins one of the entertaining stories contained in this thoroughly enjoyable edition by Thomas Reigstad, a highly respected Mark Twain scholar and Buffalo, New York, native. Professor Reigstad's specialty is Samuel Langhorne Clemens's sojourn in Buffalo from 1869 to 1871, a period of some twenty months. His scholarship about this period is well documented in his articles, lectures, and the publication of his book, *Scribblin' for a Livin': Mark Twain's Pivotal Period in Buffalo.*

This edition is a natural outgrowth of the decades Professor Reigstad spent combing through archives in Buffalo's Central Library, perusing historical and biographical scrapbooks and reading copies of the *Buffalo Express*, the newspaper co-owned and coedited by Clemens during the time he lived in the Queen City. It is only fitting that over the course of Professor Reigstad's stellar career in the Department of English at Buffalo State University and as an associate editor of *Bills Insider*—the magazine for his hometown football team, the Buffalo Bills—he also was a feature writer and copy editor at the *Buffalo Courier-Express*, a successor to Clemens's newspaper.

After reading through this marvelous collection of stories, accompanied by illustrations from five artists spanning 150 years, I had a dream of my own. Perhaps it was more of an imagining than a dream, but I tried to envision what it must have been like for the earnest and honest citizens of 1870s Buffalo, population 118,000, to open their morning paper and read these Mark Twain stories for the very first time. Or even better, what it must have been like to hear these stories read aloud to family members and friends:

> Presently up the street I heard a bony clack-clacking, and guessed it was the castanets of a serenading party. In a minute more a tall skeleton, hooded and half-clad in a tattered and mouldy shroud whose shreds were flapping about the ribby lattice-work of its person, swung by me with a stately stride, and disappeared in the gray gloom of the starlight.

Somewhere Tim Burton is nodding with great appreciation of Clemens's colorful portrayal of these ghoulish specters. "Curious Dream" is a story to treasure for its imagery, its musicality, and its comic reinvention of Ichabod Crane's experience in Sleepy Hollow.

Samuel Clemens's time in Buffalo, while brief, was highly influential in his growth as a writer. However, prior to Professor Reigstad's scholarly efforts, this period was given scant attention by past biographers. Thanks to his exhaustive research, Professor Reigstad has given us a better understanding of Clemens's growth from a newspaper correspondent writing sketches and gags for an audience of drunken miners in the Nevada territory to his early explorations into Southwestern humor and a vernacular style that might attract a middle-class audience on the East Coast.

This was a period of enormous formative personal change for Clemens, from licentious bachelorhood to adoring husband and father. Years of constant worry about money gave way to life on Delaware Avenue, the finest street in Buffalo, with a beautiful home and coachman thanks to his generous father-in-law. While this edition will substantially add to our understanding of Samuel Clemens's life, it is also a genuine joy to read these fine examples of his early writing. They give us a rare insight into the plasticity of the persona Clemens invented in Mark Twain that remains, over a hundred years since his death, a permanent part of the cultural zeitgeist of America.

—Laura Skandera Trombley, PhD, president, Southwestern University;
Lou Budd Award in Mark Twain Scholarship;
and Dixon Wecter Distinguished Professor of
American Literature, Huntington Library

ACKNOWLEDGMENTS

This book would not exist if it weren't for the talented artists who, over three centuries, created entertaining illustrative interpretations of themes, characters, and scenes in stories written by Mark Twain in the *Buffalo Express* during 1869 and 1870. I owe Twain himself for one drawing, and John Harrison Mills and True Williams—both of whom worked side by side with Twain in the late 1800s—for several others. Mills's great-grandson Ellsworth Mills II and his son Ellsworth "Chip" Mills III were extremely helpful in providing biographical and family information about their famous forebear.

I am grateful, too, for the splendid contributions of modern artists: Tom Toles and Bill Watterson for their illustrations rendered in the late 1900s and Adam Zyglis in the twenty-first century. My thanks also extend to Irene Wong and Alan Gribben, former editors of the *Mark Twain Journal*, and its current editor, Joe Fulton, for their assistance and encouragement and for generously granting permissions.

It was a treat to work as a librarian, features writer, and copy editor at the *Buffalo Courier-Express* full and part time from 1969 until its closing in 1982 with a lively bunch of fellow journalists proud to be associated with its forerunner, Twain's own *Buffalo Express*.

For any historical endeavor, archivists are indispensable. I was fortunate to rely on the expertise of Amy Pickard and Charles Alaimo of the Buffalo & Erie County Public Library's Rare Book Room; Cynthia Van Ness of the Buffalo History Museum's Research Library; Dan DiLandro, Hope Dunbar, and Susan Jaworski of Buffalo State University Archives and Special Collections; Abigail Tayse of Kenyon College's Special Collections and Archives; and Toni Engleman of the Jefferson County Historical Society.

I also received invaluable insights and assistance from Paul Weiss, Erik Brady, Michael Hiltzik, Barbara Schmidt, Gretchen Toles, Mick Cochrane, Barbara Snedecor, Darryl Brock, and Kerry Driscoll.

Many thanks to renowned Twain scholar Laura Skandera Trombley for her sparkling foreword.

To my neighbor and friend the late Martin B. Fried for his generous gift of clippings from Twain's *Buffalo Express*, several of which were scanned for this book.

Jake Bonar of Globe Pequot/North Country, a Buffalo boy at heart and, like Adam Zyglis and me, a fellow Canisius College alum, has been front and center in making this book happen. He guided its production from start to finish. Many thanks, too, to Jessica McCleary of Rowman & Littlefield and copyeditor Erin McGarvey for their expert editorial assistance.

My sons, Luke and Leif, have been behind me every step of my career-long academic journey with Twain, and I appreciate their love and continual support.

Finally, my thanks to Nancy Paschke, who has provided meticulous editorial feedback on all manner of drafts, sharing her technical skills and lovingly nudging me along at each stage of this project.

INTRODUCTION

Mark Twain (Samuel Langhorne Clemens) was a habitual doodler. He was known to draw in the margins of books and sometimes embellished his personal letters with roughly executed sketches. He fancifully inserted two renderings of elephants in his handwritten manuscript of *A Tramp Abroad*.

When his son, Langdon, was born prematurely in Buffalo in November 1870, Twain included a drawing of the baby wearing an overcoat in a birth announcement to his mother-in-law. One week later, he wrote a letter to his sister-in-law enclosing Langdon's measurements and two penciled drawings of the newborn infant sleeping, "deep in thought."

Two months earlier, Twain had designed a series of mock "fake news" headlines poking fun at the slow buildup to the Franco-Prussian War, then practiced his rudimentary artistic skills in creating a playful woodcut map of the "defense of Paris" to accompany a satirical *Buffalo Express* story about the war. Twain's *Express* war headlines and story illustration are featured in this book.

Twain learned from the works of the Southwestern humorists, a school of mid-nineteenth-century comic storytellers who popularized a style and subject unique to the "old Southwest" (which included Tennessee, Alabama, Mississippi, Missouri, and Arkansas) with entertaining tall folk tales that often contrasted new native character types such as the countrified-but-clever frontiersman and the sophisticated-but-gullible eastern Yankee interloper.

In his early magazine stories, Twain borrowed narrative techniques practiced by literary comedians and Southwestern humorists such as Augustus Baldwin Longstreet, Johnson J. Hooper, T. B. Thorpe, George W. Harris, Artemus Ward (Charles Farrar Browne), and David Ross Locke.[1]

Twain was encouraged to write his breakthrough 1865 story, "Jim Smiley and His Jumping Frog," by Ward, a popular American humorist and Twain's pal. The story's text bears several hallmarks of the Southwestern humor tradition: a frame structure; the meandering, rambling tall tale, a type of short story unique to young America; the culture contrast between a shrewd, uneducated westerner's vernacular and an easily duped, eastern stranger's grammatical correctness; verbal tricks such as hyperbole, silly similes, puns, and malapropisms; humor of physical discomfort and violence; and the climactic arrangement of details, among other devices.

After returning from his excursion to Europe and the Mideast in 1867, subsidized by the San Francisco *Daily Alta California* newspaper, Twain reshaped and added to his original travel letters to compose *The Innocents Abroad; or, The New Pilgrims' Progress*. Published just a month before he assumed his duties at the *Buffalo Express*, much of Twain's writing in *The Innocents Abroad* exhibits the array of Southwestern humor devices. Furthermore, throughout the production of the book, Twain kept tabs on the accompanying engravings being prepared by the chief artists, Roswell Morse Shurtleff and Truman W. "True" Williams.[2] Several drawings and their captions highlight key comic scenes in the narrative, scenes whose written descriptions frequently reflect elements of Southwestern humor. Twain surely had a hand in designing the images.

Once at the *Express*, Twain simply extended the successful Southwestern humor formula to his newspaper feature stories, including the handful that were illustrated.

Twain came to Buffalo with a background as an itinerant printer's apprentice, newspaper reporter, and popular lecturer (figure I.1). As soon as he took over as co-owner and managing editor of the *Buffalo Express*, he instituted sweeping changes in the newspaper. One innovation was to accompany a planned series of his Saturday feature stories with illustrations by the staff artist. Earl D. Berry, a young reporter at the *Express*, recalls that "all of the illustrations were drawn in the rough by Mr. Clemens and finished off by the woodcut artist in the composing room."[3]

This book reprints ten original humorous feature stories published by Twain in the *Buffalo Express* during 1869 and 1870, each accompanied by illustrations drawn by six artists spanning more than 150 years. There is the drawing by Twain himself, created in 1870; several by his *Express* staff artist, John Harrison Mills, done in the fall of 1869; and others by his favorite contemporary illustrator, True Williams, completed in the early 1870s, after Twain had moved from Buffalo and abandoned journalism as a career. Twain personally consulted with both Mills and Williams about the illustrations for his stories from the *Express*.

The book also includes more modern illustrations by Tom Toles, rendered in 1978; by Bill Watterson, drawn five years later; and two by Adam Zyglis, which were created in 2023 just for this book. As a bonus, the book adds two twenty-first-century caricatures of Twain, one as he looked in his early thirties in Buffalo and a second of him decades later, as a literary lion, drawn by Zyglis in 2013 and 2014. In all, more than thirty illustrations of Twain's *Express* stories are represented in *The Illustrated Mark Twain and the* Buffalo Express.

FIGURE I.1. Mark Twain, center, with colleagues David Gray, right, and George Townsend, 1871. *Image courtesy of Buffalo State University Archives,* Courier-Express *Collection*

John Harrison Mills was born in 1842 on the family farm in Bowmansville, New York, thirteen miles east of Buffalo. At age fifteen, he moved to Buffalo to learn the fine arts of engraving, sculpting, and painting. In 1862, as a Union army private in the Civil War, he was severely wounded in the Second Battle of Bull Run. Mills ultimately returned to Buffalo on crutches and joined the *Buffalo Express* staff as a proofreader, writer, and illustrator.

After Twain took over the *Express* as co-owner and managing editor in August 1869, he and Mills began a close professional and personal relationship. They both belonged to the Nameless Club, a local literary circle. Soon, Twain capitalized on Mills's artistic talent to provide drawings for his new series of humorous feature stories in Saturday editions of the *Express*. Twain hoped the innovative illustrated stories would attract more newspaper readers.

Within a few weeks, Twain's zeal for change waned. His regular Saturday feature installments ended by early October. In the end, only four stories—in August and September—were accompanied by a total of six Mills drawings. No stories in the *Buffalo Express* before or for several months after that boasted staff-drawn illustrations.

Mills's illustrations may not have even been Twain's idea. Twain implied to his moral mentor, Mary Fairbanks, that the suggestion may have come from his fellow owners George Selkirk and Josephus Larned: "But as [the drawings] cost nothing, my partners thought we might as well have them."[4]

The Twain-Mills collaboration began on Saturday, August 21, and concluded on Saturday, September 18. Twain was thirty-three years old; Mills was twenty-seven. Years later, Mills recalled his role with Twain at the *Express* as creating "the first illustrations for Mark Twain's Sketches, engraving them upon wood in 1869."[5] In a separate account, Mills referred to being "in consultation with [Twain] about those illustrations he let me make for the sketches and stories."[6]

After finishing each Saturday feature story, Twain would give Mills rough drawings of what he wanted the accompanying illustrations to look like. Mills would employ his engraving tools—likely a lozenge graver, a V-shaped graver, or a spitsticker for hatching and fine, undulating lines—to create an illustration on wooden blocks to enhance Twain's text. These blocks were then used on the printing presses in the basement of the *Express* building at 14 East Swan Street. The blocks were designed to be the same height as—and composited alongside—moveable type in page layouts so printers could produce the pages. The quality of Mills's illustrations varied, probably depending on how much lead time Twain gave him for each job.

Twain's Saturday features in the *Express* were well advertised, with front-page column-long promotions days before publication touting "a humorous sketch, illustrated." Furthermore, Twain's stories and illustrations typically occupied the first three columns of the nine-column page—prime territory when readers scanned the paper. Twain also ingeniously marketed his innovative illustrated stories in rival local newspapers. For example, one day before "Journalism in Tennessee" appeared in his own *Express*, Twain placed an advertisement of the illustrated story on page 2 of the September 3, 1869, *Buffalo Daily Courier* (figure I.2).

Each of the four Saturday features illustrated by Mills was placed on page 1, a break from the *Express*'s standard policy of printing only national and world news items on the front page.

It's been said that on multiple occasions in 1870, Mills brought his straight-back mahogany "sitter's chair" with him to Twain's splendid home (a wedding gift from his father-in-law) on Buffalo's most prestigious boulevard, Delaware Street, so that Twain could pose for a portrait. Mills left the *Express* in 1872, headed westward, and became a renowned landscape and portrait painter in Colorado for many years. He last communicated with Twain in 1887, but upon returning to Buffalo in the early 1900s, published reminiscences about their friendship.[7]

When Twain died in April 1910, Mills draped a memorial floral wreath over the portrait he had painted, then mounted in his Elmwood Avenue home. The only time

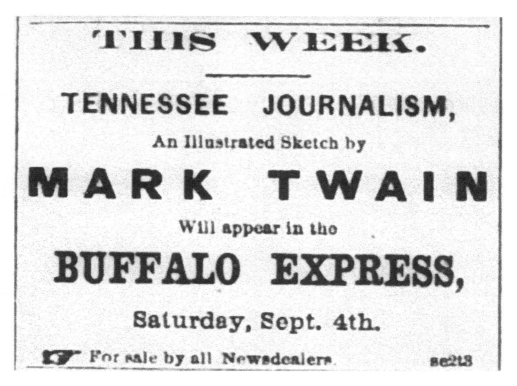

FIGURE I.2. Advertisement for illustrated "Journalism in Tennessee." *Image from the* Buffalo Daily Courier, *September 3, 1869*

the portrait was ever made public was as a supplement to an obituary of Twain in the *Buffalo Illustrated Sunday Times*.[8] Today, the portrait is owned by a Mills descendant.

Mills died in 1916, at age seventy-four, after a two-week illness and is buried in the Transit Rural Cemetery in his hometown of Bowmansville.

John Harrison Mills (figure I.3) and True Williams (figure I.4) had much in common. They were born only three years apart in rural areas of western New York, Williams in Allegany County, eighty miles southeast of Buffalo, before his family moved to Watertown in the state's North Country. Mills and Williams were both Union soldiers in the Civil War, Williams serving mostly as a topographical engineer.[9] And they were both skilled engravers and illustrators who worked elbow to elbow with Mark Twain on drawings to accompany his publications.

One thing the two artists did not share was a vulnerability to heavy drinking. Albert Bigelow Paine commented on Williams's struggle with alcoholism: "Williams was a man of great talent . . . but it was necessary to lock him in a room when industry required, with nothing more exciting than cold water as a beverage."[10] Twain himself was well aware of Williams's tendency to go on a bender in the middle of an illustrating project. In 1876 Twain wrote to William Dean Howells about Williams's "rattling good pictures" drawn for *The Adventures of Tom Sawyer* despite "murdering his genius with rum."[11]

At around the same time that Mills was providing drawings for Twain's original stories in the *Buffalo Express*, Williams was building his reputation as an illustrator for *Harper's Bazar* (as it was then spelled) and was employed by a New York illustration firm. Elisha Bliss, of the Hartford-based American Publishing Company, soon signed Williams as the lead illustrator for Twain's *The Innocents Abroad*. In early 1869, Twain wrote his fiancée, Olivia Langdon, admiring Williams's contributions: "They were drawn by a young artist of considerable talent."[12]

Later, Williams provided drawings for Twain's next book, *Roughing It*, and to *The Gilded Age* and *A Tramp Abroad*. Additionally, he was the principal illustrator for Twain's *The Adventures of Tom Sawyer* and *Sketches, New and Old*. Twain began work on *Sketches, New and Old* before he moved from Buffalo; however, he delayed publication so that it would not interfere with sales of *The Innocents Abroad*. He also reasoned that by waiting to publish *Sketches*, he would get more mileage out of previously released stories. When it was finally published in 1875, *Sketches, New and Old* was mostly old, a sort of "greatest hits" consisting of sixty-three pieces, all but seven of which had been previously published—nineteen of them in the *Buffalo Express*. Williams, in collaboration with Twain, produced 130 illustrations for *Sketches*, a popular book that has been reissued many times. (This book, *The Illustrated Mark Twain and the* Buffalo Express, reprints only the Williams drawings that accompanied five of Twain's *Express* stories so that readers may compare Williams's visual

J. HARRISON MILLS, THE ARTIST.—Page 5.

FIGURE I.3. John Harrison Mills. *Image from the* Buffalo Times, *October 23, 1904*

FIGURE I.4. Truman W. "True" Williams. *Image courtesy of the Jefferson County Historical Society, Watertown, New York*

treatments with those of the other artists spotlighted here.)

Throughout production in the summer of 1875, Twain consulted with Williams in Hartford, at times handing him roughly designed doodles in the margins of the manuscript. Indeed, it is likely that Twain suggested that Williams mirror two of Mills's original *Buffalo Express* illustrations that accompanied the Niagara Falls stories, reprinted as "Niagara" in *Sketches*. Those renderings—of commercial photographers harassing tourists and of a bemused coroner looking on as the drowning narrator futilely reaches out for assistance—are veritable carbon copies of Mills's work.

It is also apparent that while at the *Buffalo Express*, Twain instructed Mills to depict the Twain narrator in Twain's own likeness, with full, dark hair and mustache, wearing a suit, an ingenious promotional imaging gimmick inaugurated by Twain and Williams in *The Innocents Abroad* illustrations of 1869, just before Twain started at the *Buffalo Express*. As Barbara Schmidt put it, Williams created a visual brand "with caricatures of Twain with thick hair, oversized mustache and plaid trousers."[13] Williams and Twain extended this practice into the 1875 *Sketches* illustrations.

Despite debilitating health and personal problems, True Williams continued illustrating until his death at age fifty-eight in 1897. He was buried in Torode Cemetery in Hinsdale, Illinois, and later relocated to Butler Cemetery in Oak Brook, Illinois.

Fast forward to 1978. Michael A. Hiltzik, a *Buffalo Courier-Express* reporter in his mid-twenties, was surprised to discover that Mark Twain had published stories in 1869 and 1870 in the *Buffalo Express*, the forerunner of the *Courier-Express*. He had a brainstorm to reprint and write introductions to selected original Twain *Express* stories. He pitched the idea to the editor of the rotogravure supplement, the *Courier-Express Sunday* magazine.

The result was a series of four vintage Twain *Buffalo Express* stories reprinted in the *Buffalo Courier-Express Sunday* magazine between March and December 1978. Each reprint was introduced by Hiltzik and accompanied by a total of eleven new drawings by Tom Toles (figure I.5) (also in his mid-twenties at the time), listed on the magazine's masthead as "design associate."[14] Toles's drawings have never been reprinted before.

"It was great fun," Hiltzik recalls.[15] As far as directing Toles's drawings, Hiltzik said, "I'm sure I just left them to him."

Hiltzik went on to a career at the *Los Angeles Times*, sharing a Pulitzer Prize for reporting in 1999.

Toles (born in 1951) is a native of Hamburg, New York—a suburb of Buffalo—and an alumnus of the State University of New York at Buffalo. He drew for the *Buffalo Courier-Express* from 1973 to 1982, after which he began a nearly twenty-year career at the *Buffalo News* and later at the *Washington Post*, retiring in 2020. While at the *Buffalo News*, he won the Pulitzer Prize for editorial cartooning in 1990. Toles also received the 2011 Herblock Award; the Cartoonist of the Year award from *Editor and Publisher* in 2002, the National Cartoonists Society in 2003, and *The Week* magazine in 2005; and the H. L. Mencken Free Press Award for best cartoon in 1990. Readers will easily see his distinctive political cartooning style on display in the 1978 Twain *Buffalo Express* reprint series.

FIGURE I.5. Tom Toles. *Image courtesy of Nick Brengle*

Five years after the *Buffalo Courier-Express Sunday* magazine series was published, a young cartoonist named William Boyd "Bill" Watterson II (figure I.6) (born in 1958) got a gig with the *Mark Twain Journal*. While attending Kenyon College, Watterson befriended A. Robert Tenney, son of Thomas A. Tenney, the journal's editor. After graduating in 1980, and struggling as a freelancer in the early 1980s, Watterson was hired by Tenney to design the masthead for the *Journal*.[16]

FIGURE I.6. Bill Watterson. *Image from the 1980* Reveille, *courtesy of Kenyon College Special Collections and Archives*

The humorous illustration depicted a caricature of Twain, wearing his honorary Oxford gown, stogie in mouth, mortarboard set rakishly on head, scowling (figure I.7). Watterson's *Mark Twain Journal* masthead is still in use.

In 1983, Watterson collaborated with Tenney to create a series of ten postcards for the *Mark Twain Journal*. Tenney often used them to mail renewal acknowledgments to journal subscribers, and he had stacks of them available at Twain conferences to promote the journal and the Mark Twain Circle of America. One of Watterson's postcards featured an interpretation of a scene from Twain's 1870 two-part *Buffalo Express* story "Curious Dream."

On the title page of the fall 1985 *Mark Twain Journal*, editor Tenney published this announcement: "It is a pleasure to announce that Bill Watterson, whose cartoons have been appearing in the *Mark Twain Journal* since 1983, now has a very successful strip, 'Calvin and Hobbes,' appearing in over one hundred major newspapers."[17]

FIGURE I.7. *Mark Twain Journal* logo by Bill Watterson. *Image courtesy of Irene Wong,* Mark Twain Journal

Watterson retired in 1995, when his hugely popular syndicated comic strip ended. He received the National Cartoonists Society's Reuben Award twice—in 1986 and 1988. In 2014, Watterson was awarded the Grand Prix at the Angouleme International Comics Festival for his body of work.

Finally, the front and back covers of this book are caricatures of Mark Twain created by Adam Zyglis (figure I.8), editorial cartoonist at the *Buffalo News*. Zyglis (born in 1982) provided the illustrations to accompany reviews of newly published books about Twain that ran on the Sunday book pages in the *Buffalo News*. Zyglis's first drawing (this book's cover) is a caricature of Twain in his early thirties, with russet hair, flowing mustache, and hawkish nose. He's dressed in a dark suit, vest, and period tie, holding a copy of the *Buffalo Express*.[18]

Zyglis's second illustration (back cover) is also a caricature but of an older, more worldly Twain. This one depicts Twain with a wild mane of white hair, holding a pipe and wearing his trademark white suit.[19]

FIGURE I.8. Adam Zyglis. *Image courtesy of Adam Zyglis*

Zyglis also contributes two original illustrations to accompany Twain's story "Arthur." These drawings were created specifically for this book.

Zyglis, a native of western New York, grew up in rural Alden. He is an alumnus of Buffalo's Canisius College. Zyglis has been the staff cartoonist at the *Buffalo News* since 2004, succeeding Tom Toles. Like Toles, Zyglis won a Pulitzer Prize for editorial cartooning, in 2015. A past president of the Association of American Editorial Cartoonists, he published the book *You Know You're from Buffalo If . . .* in 2021.

Twain's ten *Buffalo Express* stories from 1869 and 1870 stand the test of time—their humor and subject matter are as lively now as they were then. But their entertainment value vastly increases when coupled with visual interpretations provided by six talented illustrators (including Twain himself) across three centuries.

CHAPTER ONE

SLOWLY I TURNED

Twain and Niagara Falls

O n August 14, 1869, Mark Twain officially purchased one-third ownership of the Buffalo Express *and assumed the role of managing editor. Within a week, he launched the first of a series of his humorous Saturday feature stories, titled "A Day at Niagara." This was followed the next Saturday by a second part about Niagara Falls, "English Festivities." Twain's two August 1869* Buffalo Express *stories on Niagara Falls are presented here, followed by background commentary and four accompanying illustrations from the pages of the* Express *by John Harrison Mills and six illustrations by True Williams that accompanied a combination of the two Niagara Falls stories, called "Niagara," in the 1875 collection* Mark Twain's Sketches, New and Old.

𝔅𝔲𝔣𝔣𝔞𝔩𝔬 𝔈𝔵𝔭𝔯𝔢𝔰𝔰

AUGUST 21, 1869

A DAY AT NIAGARA.

CONCERNING THE FALLS.

THE TAMED HACKMAN.

Niagara Falls is one of the finest structures in the known world. I have been visiting this favorite watering place recently, for the first time, and was well pleased. A gentleman who was with me said it was customary to be disappointed in the Falls, but that subsequent visits were sure to set that all right. He said it was so with him. He said that the first time he went the hack fares were so much higher than the Falls that the Falls appeared insignificant. But that is all regulated now. The hackmen have been tamed, and numbered, and placarded, and blackguarded, and brought into subjection to the law, and dosed with Moral Principle till they are as meek as missionaries. They are divided into two clans, now, the Regulars and the Privateers, and they employ their idle time in warning the public against each other. The Regulars are under the hotel banners, and do the legitimate at two dollars an hour, and the Privateers prowl darkly on neutral ground and pick off stragglers at half price. But there are no more outrages and extortions. That sort of thing cured itself. It made the Falls unpopular by getting into the newspapers, and whenever a public evil achieves that sort of a success for itself, its days are numbered. It became apparent that either the Falls had to be discontinued or the hackmen had to subside. They could not dam the Falls, and so they damned the hackmen. One can be comfortable and happy there now.

SIGNS AND SYMBOLS.

I drank up most of the American Fall before I learned that the waters were not considered medicinal. Why are people left in ignorance in that way? I might have gone on and ruined a fine property merely for the want of a little trifling information. And yet the sources of information at Niagara Falls are not meagre. You are sometimes in doubt there about what you ought to do, but you are seldom in doubt about what you must *not* do. No—the signs keep you posted. If an infant can read, that infant is measurably safe at Niagara Falls. In your room at the hotel you will find your course marked out for you in the most convenient way by means of placards on the wall, like these:

"Pull the bell-rope gently, but don't jerk."

"Bolt your door."

"Don't scrape matches on the wall."

"Turn off your gas when you retire."

"Tie up your dog."

"If you place your boots outside the door they will be blacked—but the house will not be responsible for their return." [This is a confusing and tanglesome proposition—because it moves you to deliberate long and painfully as to whether it will really be any object to you to have your boots blacked unless they *are* returned.]

"Give your key to the omnibus driver if you forget and carry it off with you."

Outside the hotel, wherever you wander, you are intelligently assisted by the signs. You cannot come to grief as long as you are in your right mind. But the difficulty is to *stay* in your right mind with so much instruction to keep track of. For instance:

"Keep off the grass."

"Don't climb the trees."

"Hands off the vegetables."

"Do not hitch your horse to the shrubbery."

"Visit the Cave of the Winds."

"Have your portrait taken in your carriage."

"Forty per cent. In gold levied on all pea-nuts or other Indian Curiosities purchased in Canada."

"Photographs of the Falls taken here."

"Visitors will please notify the Superintendent of any neglect on the part of employees to charge for commodities or services." [No inattention of this kind observed.]

"Don't throw stones down—they may hit people below."

"The proprietors will not be responsible for parties who jump over the Falls." [More shirking of responsibility—it appears to be the prevailing thing here.]

I always had a high regard for the Signers of the Declaration of Independence, but now they do not really seem to amount to much alongside the signers of Niagara Falls. To tell the plain truth, the multitude of signs annoyed me. It was because I noticed at last that they always happened to prohibit exactly the very thing I was just wanting to do. I desired to roll on the grass: the sign prohibited it. I wished to climb a tree: the sign prohibited it. I longed to smoke: a sign forbade it. And I was just in the act of throwing a stone over to astonish and pulverize such parties as might be picknicking below, when a sign I have just mentioned forbade that. Even that poor satisfaction was denied me, (and I a friendless orphan.)—There was no recourse, now, but to seek consolation in the flowing bowl. I drew my flask from my pocket, but it was all in vain. A sign confronted me, which said:

"No drinking allowed on these premises."

On that spot I might have perished of thirst, but for the saving words of an honored maxim that flitted through my memory at the critical moment.—"All signs fail in a dry time." Common law takes precedence of the statutes. I was saved.

THE NOBLE RED MAN.

The noble Red Man has always been a darling of mine. I love to read about him in tales and legends and romances. I love to read of his inspired sagacity; and his love of the wild free life of mountain and forest; and his grand truthfulness, his hatred of treachery, and his general nobility of character; and his stately metaphorical manner of speech; and his chivalrous love for his dusky maiden; and the picturesque pomp of his dress and accoutrement. Especially the picturesque pomp of his dress and accoutrement. When I found the shops at Niagara Falls full of dainty Indian beadwork, and stunning moccasins, and equally stunning toy figures representing human beings who carried their weapons in holes bored through their arms and bodies, and had feet shaped like a pie, I was filled with emotion. I knew that now, at last, I was going to come face to face with the Noble Red Man. A lady clerk in a shop told me, indeed, that all her grand array of curiosities were made by the Indians, and that there were plenty about the Falls, and that they were friendly and it would not be dangerous to speak to them. And sure enough, as I approached the bridge leading over to Luna Island, I came upon a noble old Son of the Forest sitting under a tree, diligently at work on a bead reticule. He wore a slouch hat and brogans, and had a short black pipe in his mouth. Thus does the baneful contact with our effeminate civilization dilute the picturesque pomp which is so natural to the Indian when far removed from us in his native haunts. I addressed the relic as follows:

"Is the Wawhoo-Wang-Wang of the Wack-a-Whack happy? Does the great Speckled Thunder sigh for the war-path, or is his heart contented with dreaming of his dusky maiden, the Pride of the Forest? Does the mighty sachem yearn to drink the blood of his enemies, or is he satisfied to make bead reticules for the papooses of the pale face? Speak, sublime relic of by-gone grandeur—venerable ruin, speak!"

The relic said:

"An is it mesilf, Dinnis Hooligan, that ye'd be takin for a bloody Injin, ye drawlin' lantern-jawed, spider-legged divil! By the piper that played before Moses, I'll ate ye!"

I went away from there.

Bye and bye, in the neighborhood of the Terrapin Tower, I came upon a gentle daughter of the aborigines, in fringed and beaded buckskin moccasins and leggins, seated on a bench with her pretty wares about her. She had just carved out a wooden chief that had a strong family resemblance to a clothes pin, and was now boring a hole through his abdomen to put his bow through. I hesitated a moment and then addressed her:

"Is the heart of the forest maiden heavy? Is the Laughing-Tadpole lonely? Does she mourn over the extinguished council-fires of her race and the vanished glory of her ancestors? Or does her sad spirit wander afar toward the hunting grounds whither her brave Gobbler-of-the-Lightnings is gone? Why is my daughter silent? Has she aught against the pale-face stranger?"

The maiden said:

"Faix, an is it Biddy Malone ye dare to be callin' names! Lave this or I'll shy your lean carcass over the catharact, ye sniveling blagyard!"

I adjourned from there, also. "Confound these Indians," I said, "they told me they were tame—but, if appearances should go for anything, I should say they were all on the war-path."

I made one more attempt to fraternise with them, and only one. I came upon a camp of them gathered in the shade of a great tree, making wampum and moccasins, and addressed them in the language of friendship:

"Noble Red Men, Braves, Grand Sachems, War-Chiefs, Squaws and High-you-Muck-a-Mucks, the pale face from the land of the setting sun greets you! You, Beneficent Polecat—you, Devourer-of-Mountains—you, Roaring-Thundergust—you, Bullyboye-with-a-Glass-Eye—the pale face from beyond the great waters greets you all! War and pestilence have thinned your ranks and destroyed your once proud nation. Poker, and seven-up, and a vain modern expense for soap, unknown to your glorious ancestors, have depleted your purses. Appropriating in your simplicity the property of others has gotten you into trouble. Misrepresenting facts, in your sinless innocence, has damaged your reputation with the soulless usurper. Trading for forty-rod whisky to enable you to get drunk and happy and tomahawk your families has played the everlasting mischief with the picturesque pomp of your dress, and here you are, in the broad light of the nineteenth century, gotten up like the ragtag and bobtail of the purlieus of New York! For shame! Remember your ancestors! Recall their mighty deeds! Remember Uncas!—and Red Jacket!—and Hole-in-the-Day!—and Horace Greeley! Emulate their achievements! Unfurl yourselves under my banner, noble savages, illustrious guttersnipes—"

"Down wid him!"

"Scoop the blagyard!"

"Hang him!"

"Burn him!"

"Dhrownd him!"

It was the quickest operation that ever was. I simply saw a sudden flash in the air of clubs, brickbats, fists, bead baskets and moccasins—a single flash, and they all appeared to hit me at once, and no two of them in the same place. In the next instant the entire tribe was upon me. They tore all the clothes off me, they broke my arms and legs, they gave me a thump that dented my head till it would hold coffee like a saucer; and to crown their disgraceful proceedings and add insult to injury, they threw me over the Horseshoe Fall and I got wet.

About ninety or a hundred feet from the top, the remains of my vest caught on a projecting rock and I was almost drowned before I could get loose. I finally fell, and brought up in a world of white foam at the foot of the Fall, whose celled and bubbly masses towered up several inches above my head. Of course I got into the eddy. I sailed round and round in it forty-four times—chasing a chip and gaining on it—each round trip a half a mile—reaching for the same bush on the bank forty-four times, and just exactly missing it by a hair's-breadth every time. At last a man walked down and sat down close to that bush, and put a pipe in his mouth, and lit a match, and followed me with one eye and kept the other on the match while he sheltered it in his hands from the wind. Presently a puff of wind blew it out. The next time I swept around he said:

"Got a match?"

"Yes—in my other vest. Help me out, please."

"Not for Joe."

When I came around again I said:

"Excuse the seemingly impertinent curiosity of a drowning man, but will you explain this singular conduct of yours?"

"With pleasure. I am the Coroner. Don't hurry on my account. I can wait for you. But I wish I had a match."

I said: "Take my place and I'll go and get you one."

He declined. This lack of confidence on his part created a coolness between us, and from that time forward I avoided him. It was my idea, in case anything happened to me, to so time the occurrence as to throw my custom into the hands of the opposition coroner over on the American side. At last a policeman came along and arrested me for disturbing the peace by yelling at people on shore for help. The Judge fined me, but I had the advantage of him. My money was with my pantaloons, and my pantaloons were with the Indians.

Thus I escaped. I am now lying in a very critical condition. At least I am lying, anyway—critical or not critical.

I am hurt all over, but I cannot tell the full extent yet, because the doctor is not done taking the inventory. He will make out my manifest this evening. However, thus far he thinks only six of my wounds are fatal. I don't mind the others.

Upon regaining my right mind, I said:

"It is an awfully savage tribe of Indians that do the bead work and moccasins for Niagara Falls, doctor. Where are they from?"

"Limerick, my son."

I shall not be able to finish my remarks about Niagara Falls until I get better.

MARK TWAIN.

Buffalo Express

AUGUST 28, 1869

ENGLISH FESTIVITIES.

AND MINOR MATTERS.

FISHING.

But seriously, (for it is well to be serious occasionally), Niagara Falls is a most enjoyable place of resort. The hotels are excellent and the prices are not at all exorbitant. The opportunities for fishing are not surpassed in the country. In fact they are not even equaled elsewhere. Because in other localities certain places in the streams are much better than others, but at Niagara one place is just as good as another, for the reason that the fish do not bite anywhere, and so there is no use in your walking five miles to fish when you can depend on being as unsuccessful nearer home. The advantages of this state of things have never heretofore been properly placed before the public.

GUIDES, PHOTOGRAPHERS AND SUCH.

The weather is cool in Summer, and the walks and drives are all pleasant and none of them fatiguing. When you start out to "do" the Falls you first drive down about a mile and pay a small sum for the privilege of looking down from a precipice into the narrowest part of the Niagara river. A railway "cut" through a hill would be as comely if it had the angry river tumbling and foaming through its bottom. You can descend a staircase here, a hundred and fifty feet down, and stand at the edge of the water. After you have done it, you will wonder why you did it, but it will then be too late. The guide will explain to you, in his blood-curdling way, how he saw the little steamer, Maid of the Mist, descend the fearful rapids—how first one paddle-box was out of sight behind the raging billows, and then the other, and at what point it was that her smokestack toppled overboard, and where her planking began to break and part asunder, and how she did finally live through the trip, after accomplishing the incredible feat of traveling seventeen miles in six minutes, or six miles in seventeen minutes, I have really forgotten which. But it was very extraordinary, anyhow. It is worth the price of admission to hear the guide tell the story nine times in succession to different parties, and never miss a word or alter a sentence or a gesture.

Then you drive over the Suspension bridge and divide your misery between the chances of smashing down two hundred feet into the river below, and the chances of having the railway train overhead smashing down on to you. Either possibility is discomforting, taken by itself—but mixed together they amount in the aggregate to positive unhappiness. On the Canada side you drive along the chasm between long ranks of photographers standing guard behind their cameras, ready to make an ostentatious frontispiece of you and your decaying ambulance and your solemn crate with a hide on it which you are expected to regard in the light of a horse, and a diminished and unimportant background of sublime Niagara—and a great many people have the ineffable effrontery or the native depravity to aid and abet this sort of crime. Any day, in the hands of these photographers you may see stately pictures of papa, and mamma, and Johnny, and Bub, and Sis, or a couple of country cousins, all smiling hideously, and all disposed in studied and uncomfortable attitudes in their carriage, and all looming up in their grand and awe-inspiring imbecility before the snubbed and diminished presentment of that majestic presence whose ministering spirits are the rainbows, whose voice is the thunder, whose awful front is veiled in clouds—who was monarch here dead and forgotten ages before this hack-full of small reptiles was deemed temporarily necessary to fill a crack in the world's unnoted myriads, and will still be monarch here ages and decades of ages after they shall have gathered themselves to their blood relations the other worms and been mingled with the unremembering dust. There is no actual harm in making Niagara a background whereon to display one's marvelous insignificance in a good strong light, but it requires a sort of superhuman self-complacency to enable one to do it.

Further along they show you where that adventurous ass, Blondin, crossed the Niagara river, with his wheelbarrow on a tight rope, but the satisfaction of it is marred by the reflection that he did not break his neck.

A DISMAL EXPERIENCE.

When you have examined the stupendous Horse Shoe Fall till you are satisfied you cannot improve on it, you return to America by the new suspension bridge, and follow up the bank to where they exhibit the Cave of the Winds. Here I followed instructions and divested myself of all my clothing and put on a water-proof jacket and overalls. This costume is picturesque, but not beautiful. A guide similarly dressed led the way down a flight of winding stairs which wound and wound, and still kept on winding long after the thing ceased to be a novelty, and then terminated long before it had begun to be a pleasure. We were then well down under the precipice, but still considerably above the level of the river. We now began to creep along flimsy bridges of a single plank, our persons shielded from perdition by a crazy wooden railing, to which I clung with both hands—not because I was afraid, but because I wanted to. Presently the descent became steeper and the bridge flimsier, and sprays from the American Fall began to rain down on us in fast-increasing sheets that soon became blinding, and after that our progress was mostly in the nature of groping. Now a furious wind began to rush out from behind the waterfall, which seemed determined to sweep us from the bridge and scatter us on the rocks and among the torrents below. I remarked that I wanted to go home. But it was too late. We were almost under the monstrous wall of water thundering down from above, and speech was in vain in the midst of such a pitiless crash of sound. In another moment the guide disappeared behind the grand deluge, and, bewildered by the thunder, driven helplessly by the wind, and smitten by the arrowy tempest of rain, I followed. All was darkness. Such a mad storming, roaring and bellowing of warring wind and water never crazed my ears before. I bent my head and seemed to receive the Atlantic on my back. The world seemed going to destruction. I could not see anything, the flood poured down so savagely. I raised my head, with open mouth, and the most of the American cataract went down my throat. If I had sprung a leak now, I had been lost. And at this moment I discovered that the bridge had ceased, and we must trust for a foothold to the slippery and precipitous rocks. I never was so scared before and survived it. But we got through at last, and emerged into the open day where we could stand in front of the laced and frothy and seething world of descending water and look at it. When I saw how much of it there was, and how fearfully in earnest it was, I was sorry I had gone behind it.

I said to the guide:

"Son, did you know what kind of an infernal place this was before you brought me down here?"

"Yes."

This was sufficient. He had known all the horror of the place, and yet he brought me there. I regarded it as deliberate arson. I then destroyed him.

ENGLISH FESTIVITIES.

I managed to find my way back alone to the place from whence I had started on this foolish enterprise, and then hurried over to Canada to avoid having to pay for the guide. At the principal hotel I fell in with the Major of the Forty-Second Fusileers and a dozen other hearty and hospitable Englishmen, and they invited me to join them in celebrating the Queen's birth-day. I said I liked all the Englishmen I had ever happened to be acquainted with, and that I, like all my countrymen, admired and honored the Queen. But I said there was one insuperable drawback—I never drank anything strong upon any occasion whatever, and I did not see how I was going to do proper and ample justice to anybody's birthday with the thin and ungenerous beverages I was accustomed to. The Major scra'ched his head and thought over the matter at considerable length; but there seemed to be no way of mastering the difficulty, and he was too much of a gentleman to suggest even a temporary abandonment of my principles. But by-and-bye he said:

"I have it. Drink soda water. As long as you never do drink anything more nutritious there isn't any impropriety in it."

And so it was settled. We met in a large parlor handsomely decorated with flags and evergreens, and seated ourselves at a board well laden with creature comforts, both solid and liquid. The toasts were happy and the speeches were good, and we kept it up until long after midnight. I never enjoyed myself more in my life. I drank thirty-eight bottles of soda-water. But do you know that that is not a reliable article for a steady drink? It is too gassy. When I got up in the morning I was full of gas and as tight as a balloon. I hadn't an article of clothing that I could wear except my umbrella.

After breakfast I found the Major making grand preparations again. I asked what it was for, and he said this was the Prince of Wales's birth-day. It had to be celebrated that evening. We celebrated it. Much against my expectations, we had another splendid time. We kept it up till some time after midnight again. I was tired of soda, and so I changed off for lemonade. I drank several quarts. You may consider lemonade better for a steady drink than soda-water, but it isn't so. In the morning it had soured on my stomach. Biting anything was out of the question—it was equivalent to lock-jaw. I was beginning to feel worn and sad, too.

Shortly after luncheon I found the Major in the midst of some more preparations. He said this was the Princess Alice's birthday. I concealed my grief.

"Who is the Princess Alice?" I asked.

"Daughter of her Majesty the Queen," the Major said.

I succumbed. That night we celebrated the Princess Alice's birth-day. We kept it up as late as usual, and really I enjoyed it a good deal. But I could not stand lemonade. I drank a couple kegs of ice water.

In the morning I had tooth-ache, and cramps, and chilblains, and my teeth were on edge from the lemonade, and I was still pretty gassy. I found the inexorable Major at it again.

"Who is this for?" I asked.

"His Royal Highness, the Duke of Edinburgh," he said.

"Son of the Queen?"

"Yes."

"And this is his birth-day—you haven't made any mistake?"

"No—the celebration comes off tonight."

I bowed before the new calamity. We celebrated the day. I drank part of a barrel of cider. Among the first objects that met my weary and jaundiced eye the next day was the Major, at his interminable preparations again. My heart was broken and I wept.

"Whom do we mourn this time?" I said.

"The Princess Beatrice, daughter of the Queen."

"Here, now," I said. "It is time to begin to enquire into this thing. How long is the Queen's family likely to hold out? Who comes next on the list?"

"Their Royal Highnesses Anne, Mary, Elizabeth, Gertrude, Augusta, William, Simon, Ferdinand, Irene, Sophia, Susannah, Socrates, Samson—"

"Hold! There is a limit to human endurance. I am only mortal. What man dare do, I dare—but he who can celebrate this family in detail, and live to tell of it is less or more than man. If you have to go through this every year, it is a mercy I was born in America, for I haven't constitution enough to be an Englishman. I shall have to withdraw from this enterprise. I am out of drinks. Out of drinks, and thirteen more to celebrate. Out of drinks, and only just on the outskirts of the family yet, as you may say. I am sorry enough to have to withdraw, but it is plain enough that it has to be done. I am full of gas and my teeth are loose, and I am wrenched with cramps, and afflicted with scurvy, and toothache, measles, mumps and lockjaw, and the cider last night has given me the cholera. Gentlemen, I mean well, but really I am not in a condition to celebrate the other thirteen. Give us a rest."

[I find, now, that it was all a dream. One avoids much dissipation by being asleep.]

MARK TWAIN.

*L*ONG BEFORE THE OLD VAUDEVILLE ROUTINE "NIAGARA FALLS . . . Slowly I Turned," Mark Twain used Niagara Falls to trigger a "violent" outpouring of writing projects.

Niagara Falls captivated Twain's creative imagination for much of his career. In one of his earliest incarnations, a fanciful story called "The First Authentic Mention of Niagara Falls: Extracts from Adam's Diary," he chooses the Falls as the setting for nothing less than the Garden of Eden. The story appears as a chapter in the 1893 anthology *The Niagara Book: A Complete Souvenir of Niagara Falls*, published in Buffalo by Underhill and Nichols.[1]

More often throughout his writing, Twain used the Falls as analogy. In *The Innocents Abroad; or, The New Pilgrims' Progress*, it serves as a measure to gauge the height of St. Peter's Basilica in Rome ("it was a good deal more than half as high as Niagara Falls").

In his 1897 tome, *Following the Equator*, Twain compares the Falls to another world wonder, the Taj Mahal. He humorously recalls his first impression of the Falls—a "beruffled little wet apron hanging out to dry"—as a huge letdown. He claims it took fifteen more visits before he could "wholesomely wonder at them for what they were, not what I expected them to be." Unlike the Taj Mahal, he said, whose divine beauty he appreciated immediately the *first* time.

In the 1905 manuscript version of *King Leopold's Soliloquy*, just five years before Twain died, he satirically describes the Belgian dictator excitedly clawing and combing "his flowing Niagara of a beard" as he rants about leaks by the press. And as a New York City resident finally witnessing a performance by the Children's Theatre for immigrants on the Lower East Side of Manhattan, Twain expressed his amazement in a gushing review during a curtain speech: "It's like a man living for a lifetime in Buffalo, eighteen miles from Niagara, and never going to see the Falls. So I had lived in New York and knew nothing about the Educational Alliance."[2]

However, it was Twain's three-day visit to Niagara Falls—his first time there in early August 1869—when he took true aim at the natural world's eighth wonder with an extended blend of reportage and fiction, comedy and ridicule.

From August 4 to 6, Twain toured Niagara Falls as part of an entourage with his future wife, Olivia Langdon of Elmira, New York, her parents, and a party of relatives and family friends. Though they stayed at the luxurious Cataract House, Twain found much about the experience to ridicule. As he strolled the grounds or traveled to the usual tourist traps, he shook off continual offers of posed photos, cheap souvenirs, and carriage taxi rides. He bemoaned how the beauty of the Falls and its grounds was marred by excessive signage, admission fees, and other commercial intrusions on its sublime natural wonder. As a reporter, Twain and his nose for news learned of the season's scandals—swindling hackmen (carriage drivers) who overcharged tourists to transport them from one destination to the other and pesky guides who badgered visitors into registering for high-priced tours. One report described how as many as twenty drivers would converge on tourists as soon as they stepped outside of their hotels. And each attraction—the Cave of the Winds, the Rapids View, Goat Island, Devil's Hole, the Whirlpool—required a costly ticket for entrance. Twain also caught wind of an upcoming circus by one "Professor Jenkins," advertising a daredevil velocipede ride atop a tightrope stretched across the Niagara gorge.

Two weeks later, newly settled in his third-floor cubbyhole office at the *Buffalo Express*, Twain launched his series of humorous Saturday features (mostly fiction, mixed with fact) with a two-part take on Niagara Falls.

His first installment, "A Day at Niagara. Concerning the Falls," followed the next Saturday by "English Festivities. And Minor Matters," shows the influence of tall-tale formulas practiced by the Southwest school of American humorists. Twain's comic toolbox includes such verbal tricks as puns, ridiculously overblown rhetoric, nubs or snappers, silly similes, climactic arrangement, and even slapstick, as when the narrator assaults his tour guide and the narrator as "inspired idiot" who invites all manner of misunderstanding and mayhem.

John Harrison Mills, Twain's illustrator at the *Express*, captured Twain's tongue-in-cheek scenes from the two installments in four drawings—a novelty for *Express* pieces at the time: the amusing predicament of the narrator after he has been thrown over the Falls (figure 1.1); the "authentic" Native American gear sold by phony vendors to gullible tourists (figure 1.2); the hack drivers and photographers who preyed on tourists (figure 1.3); and the narrator's encounter with the Cave of the Winds guide, who he felt betrayed him (figure 1.4).

"GOT A MATCH?"

FIGURE 1.1. "Got a Match?" This John Harrison Mills illustration accompanied Twain's *Buffalo Express* story "A Day at Niagara." *Image from the* Buffalo Express, *August 21, 1869*

THE CHILD OF THE FOREST.

FIGURE 1.2. "The Child of the Forest." This John Harrison Mills illustration accompanied Twain's *Buffalo Express* story "A Day at Niagara." *Image from the* Buffalo Express, *August 21, 1869*

NIAGARA AS A BACKGROUND.

FIGURE 1.3. "Niagara as a Background." This John Harrison Mills illustration accompanied Twain's *Buffalo Express* story "English Festivities." *Image from the* Buffalo Express, *August 28, 1869*

FIGURE 1.4. "I Then Destroyed Him." This John Harrison Mills illustration accompanied Twain's *Buffalo Express* story "English Festivities." *Image from the* Buffalo Express, *August 28, 1869*

"I THEN DESTROYED HIM."

Six years later, Twain approved almost identical conceptual renderings of two of Mills's four drawings—"Niagara as a Background" and "Got a Match?"—this time by artist True Williams, to accompany a reprint of the stories. Twain merged the two installments into one amalgam, which he titled simply "Niagara" and republished it in a collection of sixty-three stories he called *Sketches, New and Old* (1875).

In the *Sketches* version, Williams added six original illustrations, the first as a decorative chapter heading, filling almost a whole page, with Twain's text wrapping around the main illustration. The image shows the Twain narrator with a fishing pole and picnic basket, blithely lighting his pipe while perched precariously on a narrow ledge at the brink of the Falls (figure 1.5).

FIGURE 1.5. Decorative chapter heading; illustration by True Williams for Twain's story "Niagara." *Image from* Mark Twain's Sketches, New and Old *(Hartford, CT: American Publishing Company, 1875), 63*

The next, the hack drivers and photographers who prey on tourists (figure 1.6), is similar in concept to Mills's 1869 drawing.

The third illustration shows the soaked narrator's harrowing walk over a flimsy plank bridge during the Cave of the Winds tour (figure 1.7).

FIGURE 1.6. Carriage drivers and photographers; illustration by True Williams for Twain's story "Niagara." *Image from* Mark Twain's Sketches, New and Old *(Hartford, CT: American Publishing Company, 1875), 65*

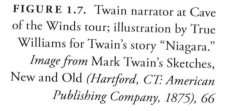

FIGURE 1.7. Twain narrator at Cave of the Winds tour; illustration by True Williams for Twain's story "Niagara." *Image from* Mark Twain's Sketches, New and Old *(Hartford, CT: American Publishing Company, 1875), 66*

A fourth shows the narrator interfering with a peddler of ersatz beadwork who is posing as a Native American (figure 1.8).

FIGURE 1.8. Twain narrator harassing beadwork vendor; illustration by True Williams for Twain's story "Niagara." *Image from* Mark Twain's Sketches, New and Old *(Hartford, CT: American Publishing Company, 1875), 68*

The fifth drawing is of the self-proclaimed "gentle daughter of the aborigines" selling "authentic" wood carvings, whose brogue reveals her true Irish identity (figure 1.9).

FIGURE 1.9. Twain exposing fake Native American vendor; illustration by True Williams for Twain's story "Niagara." *Image from* Mark Twain's Sketches, New and Old *(Hartford, CT: American Publishing Company, 1875), 69*

The last illustration, modeled after a Mills idea, is of a coroner refusing to aid the Twain narrator after he is tossed over the Falls (figure 1.10).

FIGURE 1.10. Twain narrator swirling in whirlpool at base of Niagara Falls; illustration by True Williams for Twain's story "Niagara." *Image from* Mark Twain's Sketches, New and Old *(Hartford, CT: American Publishing Company, 1875), 71*

CHAPTER TWO

THE PRINCE AND THE PRESS

Twain Makes a Royal Flush

W hen word spread on September 27, 1869, that Britain's young Prince Arthur was making a spur-of-the-moment visit to Buffalo, the local press swung into action. Mark Twain joined a gaggle of other hastily gathered reporters to write up the prince's impromptu tour of the city. Turns out that Twain was more offended than impressed by the prince. Twain's account in the Express the next day sarcastically reflects his disdain for Prince Arthur's snooty attitude. Reports published in rival Buffalo newspapers were objective and fact based, with no humor infused in them. Twain's story, "Arthur," appears below, followed by background commentary and two brand-new illustrations drawn by Adam Zyglis exclusively for this book in 2023, the only illustrations ever rendered for this entertaining Express story by Twain.

𝔅𝔲𝔣𝔣𝔞𝔩𝔬 𝔈𝔵𝔭𝔯𝔢𝔰𝔰

SEPTEMBER 28, 1869

ARTHUR.

We seldom have a live prince to chronicle, and though we have little to chronicle about this one that has been visiting us a moment yesterday, we calculate to make the most of him, anyhow. He is one of the sons of the Queen of England, but *which* one we cannot possibly get at. But being the son of a Queen, and especially the Queen of one of the greatest empires on earth, the *reveille* of whose military garrisons "follows the sun around the globe," and rattles and clatters on British territory all the time; and being a young personage whose ancestors have always sat on thrones, and whose crowns glitter in far-reaching procession back through history and the mists of tradition for a thousand years; whose blue imperial blood is filtered down to him in a more or less diluted state. From Plantagenets, Tudors, Stewarts, Dutchmen, Germans, and all sorts of people whose sires look out from the shadows of antiquity in questionable shapes as Scandinavian, pirates stirring up unoffending Normandy—stout old William, the Conqueror, stirring up the good Saxons eight hundred years ago—Richard of the Lion Heart doing fabulous feats of valor at the head of his crusading hosts in Holy Land—the knightly Black Prince, of romantic memory—stage-ridden Richard III, whose crime of smothering his infant nephews was insignificant compared to the misery he has doomed the world to suffer in theatres, watching McKean Buchanan and similar artists cavort through the tragedy that bears his name—the old "original Jacobs" of the divorce policy, Henry VIII, who missed his opportunity when he was born in Windsor Castle instead of Chicago—the stately old Elizabeth, the "virgin queen" of questionable virginity—Charles the Martyr, Charles the Fop, James the Bigot, and that nice invoice of Georges, who began as semi-savages and ended mildly civilized but with crazed brain—we repeat that when we capture a youth of such illustrious antecedents as this young Prince Arthur is graced withal, we feel it a Christian duty to make the most of him.

THE PRINCE'S MOVEMENTS

But it is not possible to spread him over much ground, from the fact that he did not stay with us long, and did nothing but what any common mortal might have done, while he did stay—for he only took lunch, and then got out of the United States again, right away.

He and his party arrived in this city at one o'clock yesterday afternoon on a special train from Niagara Falls.

No notice was given of his coming, and there was but a small crowd at the depot, and that consisted in a large part of passengers who came in on the regular, one minute ahead of the extra.

On alighting from the car the Prince gave his arm to Lady Young, and the party proceeded at once to the carriages.

The first carriage was occupied by the Prince, Lady Young, Colonel Roland and Colonel Elphinstone.

In the second carriage were the Governor General, Sir Henry Young, Miss Bush, Colonel Turville, and Colonel McNiell.

Just as the carriages started the crowd indulged in quite a hearty cheer.

The party proceeded at once to the Tifft House for lunch.

There was no crowd about the hotel, for nobody knew so august a visitor was expected. A luncheon was set in parlors No. 1 and 2, at the hotel, and the party as above named partook of it, assisted by five invited guests—ex-President Fillmore, British Consul Hemans, Col. Pickard, and two ladies.

Mr. Fillmore was the most distinguished American to be had, and he was appointed to preside over the affair. A colored man in white kids stood guard at the door and kept strict blockade against reporters and other hunters after the British Lion. A dozen young misses, not old enough to marry, but plenty old enough to have a maidenly curiosity about princes, stayed around in an unintentional sort of way, and seized the occasional opportunities that offered to take a peep.

THE REST OF IT

His Highness is a slim-breasted youth of nineteen, with dainty side whiskers, very light hair parted three inches above his left ear, and with the royal nose and shelving forehead of the Georges. He made no remarks to us; did not ask us to dinner; walked right by us just the same as if he didn't see us; never inquired our opinion about any subject under the sun; and when his luncheon was over got into his carriage and drove off in the coolest way in the world without ever saying a word—and yet he could not know but that that was the last time he might ever see us. But if he can stand it, we can.

Prince Arthur looks pleasant and agreeable, however. He has a good, reliable, tenacious appetite, of about two-king capacity. He was the last man to lay down his knife and fork.

This is absolutely all that England's princely son did in Buffalo—absolutely all! We shall go on and make all the parade we can about it, but none of his acts in Buffalo were noisy enough for future historical record. It was *Veni, Vidi, Vici*, with him. He came—he saw that lunch—he conquered it.

The party took carriages and drove through Main and Ohio streets to the Niagara elevator; glanced at it, and at another; drove through half a dozen of the principal streets and out in the neighborhood of Fort Porter; drove back in front of the hotel and waited till one of the party went in for a moment—to pay the bill or make a royal present to somebody, likely; drove down and stopped a moment in front of Mr. Fillmore's; and then they rattled off to the depot, took a special train, of one Director's car, and left for the Clifton House, Niagara Falls. Time on American soil, four hours and a half—two and a half of which were spent on the sacred soil of Buffalo. The party were in something of a hurry to get away and prepare for a hunt in the vicinity of Long Point in the morning.

Prince Arthur's visit was unexpected, and his presence almost unknown while he remained. So his movements were free and unembarrassed by the throng of curious citizens that might have appeared on the streets if they had known what royal Jehu it was who was driving so furiously through our thoroughfares.

It is usual for princes to "express themselves well pleased with their visit." No doubt this one did—but not to us.

NOT COMING TO THE FAIR

His Royal Highness is invited to be present at the opening of the Fair—and if he could have accepted, he would have been cordially received and kindly welcomed. The following is the

CORRESPONDENCE:
International Industrial Exhibition,
Buffalo, September 27, 1869

To His Royal Highness Prince Arthur,

May it please your Royal Highness, on behalf of the Board of Managers and Officers of the International Industrial Exhibition, I would most respectfully and cordially invite your Royal Highness and your distinguished suite to attend the inaugural ceremonies of the Exhibition, which take place in this city on the 6th proximo. The high esteem in which the royal family you represent is held in the United States assures you of a generous welcome to the Empire State.

I am, with great respect,
Your obedient servant,
DAVID BEEL,
President International Industrial Exhibition

[REPLY]

NIAGARA, September 27, 1869

DEAR SIR: I am desired by H.R.H., Prince Arthur, to acknowledge the receipt of your letter of this date, inviting His Royal Highness to attend the inaugural ceremonies of the Industrial Exhibition, which is to be held in Buffalo on the 6th of October.

His Royal Highness fully appreciates the kindness of the invitation, but desires me to say that he regrets very much that a previous engagement at Kingston will prevent his attending this very interesting exhibition.

Believe me,
Yours faithfully,
H. ELPHINSTONE
Col. R.E., Governor to His Royal Highness

*A*LTHOUGH MARK TWAIN CRITICIZED AMERICAN POLITICS AND politicians, his dislike of monarchal rule was even more intense. His *Prince and the Pauper* and *A Connecticut Yankee in King Arthur's Court* dramatize the evils of monarchy and indict the caste systems of nobility and aristocratic privilege, particularly in Great Britain. One of Twain's earliest satires of British royalty was "Arthur," published in the *Buffalo Express* on September 28, 1869.

Prince Arthur was the seventh of Queen Victoria's nine children. In 1869, as a nineteen-year-old, he toured Canada for two months. In his September 25 "People and Things" column, Twain inserted a snide entry on the tour: "Prince Arthur has been making presents to Canadian dignitaries. More trouble brewing." Two days later, the *Express* announced that a delegation from Buffalo would call on the prince in Niagara Falls and invite him to Buffalo's International Fair, scheduled for October.

Instead, the prince and his retinue made a surprise pit stop in Buffalo on the same day.

When Arthur's special train pulled into Buffalo's Erie Street depot around 1:00 p.m. virtually unannounced, he was accompanied by his private tutor, Colonel Howard Craufurd Elphinstone; a large party of Canadian and British dignitaries; and two attractive young women from Philadelphia. Local officials quickly swung into action to give young Arthur a royal red-carpet welcome.

Several carriages whisked the prince and his travel guests to a hastily arranged but sumptuous meal in an exclusive dining hall at the city's posh hotel, the Tifft House on Main Street. A separate carriage packed with a pool of reporters from the *Buffalo Courier*, the *Commercial Advertiser*, and the *Express* (including Twain) tagged along behind the official procession. Buffalo's elder statesman, former US president

Millard Fillmore and Henry William Hemans, the British consul for the United States at Buffalo, scrambled to help host the last-minute luncheon.

Once at the Tifft House, the journalists were again kept at bay, allowed only to peer in at the elite diners through the banquet room's French doors.

But Twain saw enough of the prince to form some impressions, dripping with satire.

After an hour of eating, toasting, and imbibing, the caravan of carriage goers, now led by one carrying Fillmore and Hemans, was driven south on Main toward Ohio Street so that the prince could inspect the city's pride and joy—the new Niagara grain elevator, one of twenty-five such impressive structures that made Buffalo the largest grain port of the time.

From there, the excursion of carriages—again, with reporters bringing up the rear—headed back to Main, turning west onto Niagara so that Fillmore could show off his own mansion. The tour continued so that the prince and his underlings could further ogle the splendid residences of Buffalo's nouveau riche that lined Delaware Street, its grandest avenue, and closed by passing the opulent twenty-two-thousand-square-foot home, occupying five acres, owned by William G. Fargo, a former mayor and founder of the American Express Company and Wells Fargo.

The prince's brief three-hour stay in Buffalo ended when his special train departed for the return trip to Niagara Falls at 4:00.

Twain's *Express* story the next day ridiculed Arthur's lineage, his healthy appetite ("It was *Veni, Vidi, Vici,* with him. He came—he saw that lunch—he conquered it."), his haughtiness, and his seeming disinterest in Buffalo's attractions.

Being Mark Twain, he extended his irreverent treatment to the royal family. In the following day's *Express*, he introduced a reprinted article from *Packard's Monthly*: "Apropos of the Prince's visit to Buffalo, it might interest the public to know what his mother looked like in her prime." The *Packard* piece described Queen Victoria as "short and dumpy at 32."

Twain must have resented being relegated to join a scrum of journalists denied access to the prince and forced to trail the arrogant teenager at a distance. In a slightly bitter letter to his moral mentor, Mary Fairbanks, Twain privately echoed his public comic sarcasm toward the prince and his Buffalo visit:

> We had Prince Arthur in town a little while this afternoon, but he never called on me, & so I threw myself back on my dignity & never called on *him*. He is too stuck-up, altogether. I am on too familiar terms with his betters in Russia to go browsing around after mere princes. I let him skin around town as long as he wanted to & skin out again when he got ready. But I wrote him up.[1]

Ironically, nearly forty years later, when Oxford University awarded Twain an honorary doctor of letters, he stood alongside Prince Arthur, Duke of Connaught and Strathearn, at the ceremony. It's a cinch that Twain did not bring up his old *Express* story.

Even though "Arthur" was unsigned when it appeared in the 1869 *Buffalo Express*, it was clearly written by Twain. Inexplicably, this entertaining satire was not reprinted for nearly 115 years.[2] It was even omitted from a 1999 collection of his *Express* contributions.[3]

The story was never accompanied by an illustration until 2023, when Adam Zyglis created his renderings exclusively for this book. Here's how he described the experience: "They were fun to produce. . . . It seemed the prince ate and left, so these are the scenes I got. I researched Arthur and made sure it resembles him from old photos I found, as well as Millard Fillmore."[4]

Indeed, the first illustration (figure 2.1) shows the haughty young prince and ex-president Fillmore chowing down at the exclusive luncheon while a grumpy Twain takes notes off to the side. Zyglis's rendering interprets Twain's satirical account of Arthur's "royal nose and shelving forehead of the Georges."

FIGURE 2.1. Twain taking notes on Prince Arthur's luncheon; illustration by Adam Zyglis for Twain's *Buffalo Express* story "Arthur." *Image courtesy of Adam Zyglis, 2023*

The second illustration (figure 2.2) catches the prince's haste to round up his retinue and get out of town after the meal and tour, again with a crabby Twain recording the departure while inhaling the dust of the prince's rushing royal carriage.

FIGURE 2.2. Twain reporting on Prince Arthur's hasty departure; illustration by Adam Zyglis for Twain's *Buffalo Express* story "Arthur." *Image courtesy of Adam Zyglis, 2023*

CHAPTER THREE

YELLOW JOURNALISM

Mark Twain Sees Red

———

*B*arely three weeks into his tenure at the Buffalo Express, *Twain published his third feature story, "Journalism in Tennessee," a parody of the sensational journalism of his day. The story is reprinted here, followed by explanatory comments and the only illustration by John Harrison Mills accompanying the 1869* Express *story, along with three by True Williams that appeared in* Mark Twain's Sketches, New and Old *(1875).*

———

𝔅𝔲𝔣𝔣𝔞𝔩𝔬 𝔈𝔵𝔭𝔯𝔢𝔰𝔰

SEPTEMBER 4, 1869

JOURNALISM IN TENNESSEE

The editor of the Memphis "Avalanche" swoops thus mildly down upon a correspondent who posted him as a Radical: "While he was writing the first word, the middle word, dotting his i's, crossing his t's, and punching his period, he knew he was concocting a sentence that was saturated with infamy and reeking with falsehood."

—"Exchange"

I was told by the physician that a Southern climate would improve my health, and so I went down to Tennessee and got a berth on the *Morning Glory and Johnson County War-Whoop*, as associate editor. When I went on duty I found the chief editor sitting tilted back in a three-legged chair with his feet on a pine table. There was another pine table in the room, and another afflicted chair, and both were half buried under newspapers and scraps of manuscript. There was a wooden box of sand, sprinkled with cigar stubs and "old soldiers," and a stove with a door hanging by its upper hinge. The chief editor had a long-tailed black cloth frock coat on, and white linen pants. His boots were small and neatly blacked. He wore a ruffled shirt, a large seal ring, a standing collar of obsolete pattern and a checkered neckerchief with the ends hanging down. Date of costume, about 1848. He was smoking a cigar and trying to think of a word. And in trying to think of a word, and in pawing his hair for it, he had rumpled his locks a good deal. He was scowling fearfully, and I judged that he was concocting a particularly knotty editorial. He told me to take the exchanges and skim through them and write up the "Spirit of the Tennessee Press," condensing into the article all of their contents that seemed of interest.

I wrote as follows:

"SPIRIT OF THE TENNESSEE PRESS.

"The editors of the *Semi-Weekly Earthquake* evidently labor under a misapprehension with regard to the Ballyhack railroad. It is not the object of the company to leave Buzzardville off to one side. On the contrary they consider it one of the most important points along the line, and consequently can have no desire to slight it. The gentlemen of the *Earthquake* will of course take pleasure in making the correction.

"John W. Blossom, Esq., the able editor of the *Higginsville Thunderbolt and Battle Cry of Freedom*, arrived in the city yesterday. He is stopping at the Van Buren House.

"We observe that our contemporary of the Mud Springs *Morning Howl* has fallen into the error of supposing that the election of Van Werter is not an established fact, but he will have discovered his mistake before this reminder reaches him, no doubt. He was doubtless misled by incomplete election returns.

"It is pleasant to note that the city of Blathersville is endeavoring to contract with some New York gentlemen to pave its well nigh impassable streets with Nicholson pavement. But it is difficult to accomplish a desire like this since Memphis got some New Yorkers to do a like service for her and then declined to pay for it. However the *Daily Hurrah* still urges the measure with ability, and seems confident of ultimate success.

"We are pained to learn that Col. Bascom, chief editor of the *Dying Shriek for Liberty*, fell in the street a few evenings since and broke his leg. He has lately been suffering with debility, caused by over-work and anxiety on account of sickness in his family, and it is supposed that he fainted from the exertion of walking too much in the sun."

I passed my manuscript over to the chief editor for acceptance, alteration or destruction. He glanced at it and his face clouded. He ran his eye down the pages, and his countenance grew portentous. It was easy to see that something was wrong. Presently he sprang up and said:

"Thunder and lightning! Do you suppose I am going to speak of those cattle that way? Do you suppose my subscribers are going to stand such gruel as that? Give me the pen!"

I never saw a pen scrape and scratch its way so viciously, or plough through another man's verbs and adjectives so relentlessly. While he was in the midst of his work somebody shot at him through the open window and marred the symmetry of his ear.

"Ah," said he, "that is that scoundrel Smith, of the *Moral Volcano*—he was due yesterday." And he snatched a navy revolver from his belt and fired. Smith dropped, shot in the thigh. The shot spoiled Smith's aim, who was just taking a second chance, and he crippled a stranger. It was me. Merely a finger shot off.

Then the chief editor went on with his erasures and interlineations. Just as he finished them a hand-grenade came down the stove pipe, and the explosion shivered the stove into a thousand fragments. However, it did no further damage, except that a vagrant piece knocked a couple of my teeth out.

"That stove is utterly ruined," said the chief editor.

I said I believed it was.

"Well, no matter—don't want it this kind of weather. I know the man that did it. I'll get him. Now *here* is the way this stuff ought to be written."

"SPIRIT OF THE TENNESSEE PRESS.

"The inveterate liars of the *Semi-Weekly Earthquake* are evidently endeavoring to palm off upon a noble and chivalrous people another of their vile and brutal falsehoods with regard to that most glorious conception of the nineteenth century, the Ballyhack railroad. The idea that Buzzardville was to be left off at one side originated in their own fulsome brains—or rather in the settlings which *they* regard as brains. They had better swallow this lie, and not stop to chew it, either, if they want to save their abandoned, reptile carcasses the cowhiding they so richly deserve.

"That ass, Blossom of the Higginsville *Thunderbolt and Battle-Cry of Freedom*, is down here again, bumming his board at the Van Buren.

"We observe that the besotted blackguard of the Mud Springs *Morning Howl* is giving out, with his usual propensity for lying, that Van Werter is not elected. The heaven-born mission of journalism is to disseminate truth—to eradicate error—to educate, refine and elevate the tone of public morals and manners, and make all men more gentle, more virtuous, more charitable, and in all ways better, and holier and happier—and yet this black-hearted villain, this hell-spawned miscreant, prostitutes his great office persistently to the dissemination of falsehood, calumny, vituperation and degrading vulgarity. His paper is notoriously unfit to take into the people's homes, and ought to be banished to the gambling hells and brothels where the mass of reeking pollution which does duty as its editor, lives and moves, and has his being.

"Blathersville wants a Nicholson pavement—it wants a jail and a poor-house more. The idea of a pavement in a one-horse town with two gin-mills and a blacksmith shop in it, and that mustard-plaster of a newspaper, the *Daily Hurrah*! Better borrow of Memphis, where the article is cheap. The crawling insect, Buckner, who edits the *Hurrah*, is braying about this pavement business with his customary loud-mouthed imbecility, and imagining that he is talking sense. Such foul, mephitic scum as this verminous Buckner, are a disgrace to journalism.

"That degraded ruffian, Bascom, of the *Dying Shriek for Liberty*, fell down and broke his leg yesterday—pity it wasn't his neck. He says it was "debility caused by overwork and anxiety!" It was debility caused by trying to lug six gallons of forty-rod whiskey around town when his hide is only gauged for four, and anxiety about where he was going to bum another six. He "fainted from the exertion of walking too much in the sun!" And well he might say that—but if he would walk *straight* he would get just as far and not have to walk half as much. For years the pure air of this town has been rendered perilous by the deadly breath of this perambulating pestilence, this pulpy bloat, this steaming, animated tank of mendacity, gin and profanity, this Bascom! Perish all such from out the sacred and majestic mission of journalism!"

"Now *that* is the way to write—peppery and to the point. Mush-and-milk journalism gives me the fan-tods."

About this time a brick came through the window with a splintering crash, and gave me a considerable jolt in the middle of the back. I moved out of range—I began to feel in the way. The chief said:

"That was the Colonel, likely. I've been expecting him for two days. He will be up, now, right away."

He was correct. The "Colonel" appeared in the door a moment afterward, with a dragoon revolver in his hand. He said:

"Sir, have I the honor of addressing the white-livered poltroon who edits this mangy sheet?"

"You have—be seated, Sir—be careful of the chair, one of the legs is gone. I believe I have the pleasure of addressing the blatant, black-hearted scoundrel, Col. Blatherskite Tecumseh?"

"The same. I have a little account to settle with you. If you are at leisure, we will begin."

"I have an article on the 'Encouraging Progress of Moral and Intellectual Development in America' to finish, but there is no hurry. Begin."

Both pistols rang out their fierce clamor at the same instant. The chief lost a lock of hair, and the Colonel's bullet ended its career in the fleshy part of my thigh. The Colonel's left shoulder was clipped a little. They fired again. Both missed their men this time, but I got my share, a shot in the arm. At the third fire both gentlemen were wounded slightly, and I had a knuckle chipped. I then said I believed I would go out and take a walk, as this was a private matter and I had a delicacy about participating in it further. But both gentlemen begged me to keep my seat and assured me that I was not in the way. I had thought differently, up to this time.

They then talked about the elections and the crops a while, and I fell to tieing up my wounds. But presently they opened fire again with animation, and every shot took effect—but it is proper to remark that five out of the six fell to my share. The sixth one mortally wounded the Colonel, who remarked, with fine humor, that he would have to say good morning, now, as he had business up town. He then inquired the way to the undertaker's and left. The chief turned to me and said:

"I am expecting company to dinner and shall have to get ready. It will be a *favor* to me if you will read proof and attend to the customers."

I winced a little at the idea of attending to the customers, but I was too bewildered by the fusillade that was still ringing in my ears to think of anything to say. He continued:

"Jones will be here at 3. Cowhide him. Gillespie will call earlier, perhaps—throw him out of the window. Ferguson will be along about 4—kill him. That is all for to-day, I believe. If you have any odd time, you may write a blistering article on the police—give the Chief Inspector rats. The cowhides are under the table, weapons in the drawer—ammunition there in the corner—lint and bandages up there in the pigeon-holes. In case of accident, go to Lancet, the surgeon, down stairs. He advertises—we take it out in trade."

He was gone. I shuddered. At the end of the next three hours I had been through perils so awful that all peace of mind and all cheerfulness had gone from me. Gillespie had called, and thrown *me* out of the window. Jones arrived promptly, and when I got ready to do the cowhiding, he took the job off my hands. In an encounter with a stranger, not in the bill of fare, I had lost my scalp. Another stranger, by the name of Thompson, left me a mere wreck and ruin of chaotic rags. And at last, at bay in the corner, and beset by an infuriated mob of editors, blacklegs, politicians and desperadoes, who raved and swore and flourished their weapons about my head till the air shimmered with glancing flashes of steel, I was in the act of resigning my berth on the paper when the chief arrived, and with him a rabble of charmed and enthusiastic friends. Then ensued a scene of riot and carnage as no human pen, or steel one either, could describe. People were shot, probed, dismembered, blown up, thrown out of the window. There was a brief tornado of murky blasphemy, with a confused and frantic war-dance glimmering through it, and then all was over. In five minutes there was silence, and the gory chief and I sat alone and surveyed the sanguinary ruin that strewed the floor around us. He said:

"You'll like this place when you get used to it." I said:

"I'll have to get you to excuse me. I think maybe I might write to suit you, after a while, as soon as I had had some practice and learned the language—I am confident I could. But to speak the plain truth, that sort of energy of expression has its inconveniences, and a man is liable to interruption. You see that, yourself. Vigorous writing is calculated to elevate the public, no doubt, but then I don't like to be left here to wait on the customers. The experiences are novel, I grant you, and entertaining, too, after a fashion, but they are not judiciously distributed. A gentleman shoots at you, through the window, and cripples *me*, a bomb-shell comes down the stove-pipe for your gratification, and sends the stove door down *my* throat, a friend drops in to swap compliments with you, and freckles *me* with bullet holes till my skin won't hold my principles, you go to dinner, and Jones comes with his cowhide, Gillespie throws me out of the window. Thompson tears all my clothes off, and an entire stranger takes my scalp with the easy freedom of an old acquaintance, and in less than five minutes all the blackguards in the country arrive in their war paint and proceed to scare the rest of me to death with their tomahawks. Take it altogether, I never have had such a spirited time in all my life as I have had to-day. No. I like you, and I like your calm, unruffled way of explaining things to the customers, but you see I am not used to it. The Southern heart is too impulsive—Southern hospitality is too lavish with the stranger. The paragraphs which I have written to-day, and into whose cold sentences your masterly hand has infused the fervent spirit of

Tennessee journalism, will wake up another nest of hornets. All that mob of editors will come—and they will come hungry, too, and want somebody for breakfast. I shall have to bid you adieu. I decline to be present at these festivities. I came South for my health—I will go back on the same errand, and suddenly. Tennessee journalism is too stirring for me." After which, we parted, with mutual regret, and I took apartments at the hospital.

MARK TWAIN.

MARK TWAIN ARRIVED IN BUFFALO WITH SEVERAL YEARS' EXPERI- ence as a newspaperman in the old Wild West.

He had started as a reporter in a Nevada territory mining town full of brawling, saloons, brothels, duels, and colorful personalities conducive to writing that stretched the truth. Later in his career, he often wrote of the South's extremist tendency to settle disputes with shootings, stabbings, or lynchings.

One of Twain's *Buffalo Express* editorial duties was to pore over the stacks of daily newspaper exchanges for two- or three-line news briefs that he could infuse with satire and insert in his "People and Things" column. An entry from his August 24, 1869, column announces a convention of Georgia editors whose "revolvers and bowie-knives have been transported thither" ahead of time and suggests that Atlanta undertakers should "let their funerals to the lowest bidder."

Another exchange item around the same time, about a Memphis editor who intentionally fudges the truth, inspired Twain to address two favorite themes: excessive violence in the Reconstruction South and sensational journalism. The result was Twain's third illustrated Saturday feature, "Journalism in Tennessee," published on September 4, 1869.

Twain uses the frame (story-within-a-story) technique. A serious, gentlemanly Northern journalist (the outside narrator) goes to Tennessee for his health and is exposed to the raucous Southern brand of distorted newspaper writing at the expense of his physical and mental well-being. By the end of his brief, violent tenure on a salacious Southern paper, he is hospitalized before retreating to safety and professional journalism back North—a classic Twain recipe for comic contrasts.

The narrator's unethical Southern editor in chief does editing violence to his new hire's objective reporting, while the Northerner also suffers physical violence at the hands of unhappy readers who have been victimized in print by libelous untruths aimed only at increasing subscriptions.

In a series of escalating mob assaults on the news office, irate readers not only shoot, maim, whip, and defenestrate the narrator but also wreck the news building. "Journalism in Tennessee" was a parable on irresponsible journalism and the chaos of Southern Reconstruction writ large. Dark humor, indeed.

For this piece, Twain's *Express* colleague John Harrison Mills created one drawing. It depicts the mayhem when an aggrieved reader tosses a "hand-grenade" down the stovepipe and blasts the office stove to smithereens. Mills and Twain used a line from the story as a caption: "That stove is utterly ruined" (figure 3.1).

True Williams produced three illustrations to accompany the reprinted "Journalism in Tennessee" in *Sketches, New and Old* (1875). A nearly full-page drawing on the title page shows the vengeful Colonel Blatherskite Tecumseh drawing his revolver on the offensive editor in chief (figure 3.2); the "scene of riot and carnage" as the narrator fends for himself against a bloodthirsty crowd of wronged readers (figure 3.3); and the narrator's hospital bed in the aftermath of his editorial office wounds (figure 3.4).

"THAT STOVE IS UTTERLY RUINED."

FIGURE 3.1. "That Stove Is Utterly Ruined." This John Harrison Mills illustration accompanied Twain's *Buffalo Express* story "Journalism in Tennessee." *Image from the* Buffalo Express, *September 4, 1869*

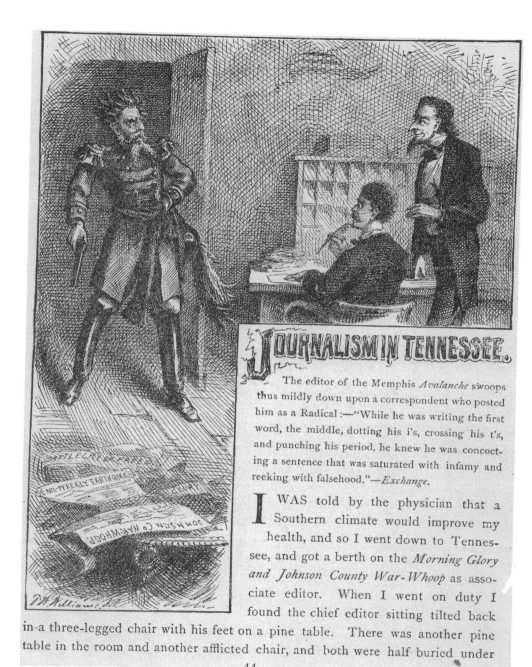

JOURNALISM IN TENNESSEE.

The editor of the Memphis *Avalanche* swoops thus mildly down upon a correspondent who posted him as a Radical :—"While he was writing the first word, the middle, dotting his i's, crossing his t's, and punching his period, he knew he was concocting a sentence that was saturated with infamy and reeking with falsehood."—*Exchange*.

I WAS told by the physician that a Southern climate would improve my health, and so I went down to Tennessee, and got a berth on the *Morning Glory and Johnson County War-Whoop* as associate editor. When I went on duty I found the chief editor sitting tilted back in a three-legged chair with his feet on a pine table. There was another pine table in the room and another afflicted chair, and both were half buried under

44

FIGURE 3.2. Decorative chapter heading; illustration by True Williams for Twain's story "Journalism in Tennessee." *Image from* Mark Twain's Sketches, New and Old (*Hartford, CT: American Publishing Company, 1875), 44*

FIGURE 3.3. Narrator amid chaos of disgruntled newspaper readers; illustration by True Williams for Twain's story "Journalism in Tennessee." *Image from* Mark Twain's Sketches, New and Old *(Hartford, CT: American Publishing Company, 1875), 49*

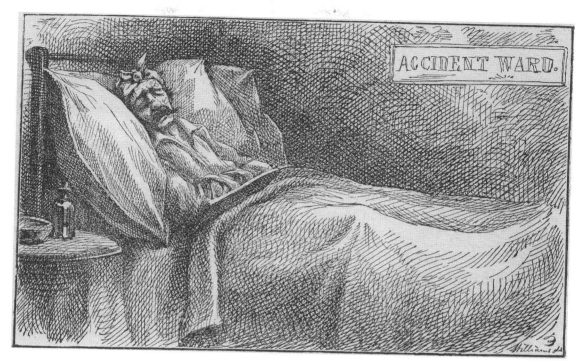

FIGURE 3.4. Narrator recovering from newsroom injuries; illustration by True Williams for Twain's story "Journalism in Tennessee." *Image from* Mark Twain's Sketches, New and Old *(Hartford: American Publishing Company, 1875), 50*

CHAPTER FOUR

FAMOUS LAST WORDS

Insert Twain's Foot in Mouth

———

hen Twain's "The Last Words of Great Men" appeared in September 1869 as a Saturday feature story in the Express, *he did not bother asking his colleague, staff artist Mills, for a drawing; however, 109 years later, a young Tom Toles of the* Buffalo Courier-Express *(the successor to Twain's own paper) rose to the task and created four of his own to delight readers of the late twentieth century with witty illustrations to accompany Twain's fanciful story about alleged deathbed statements of celebrities. The story is here, with explanatory commentary, and the Toles renderings.*

———

𝔅𝔲𝔣𝔣𝔞𝔩𝔬 𝔈𝔵𝔭𝔯𝔢𝔰𝔰

SEPTEMBER 11, 1869

THE LAST WORDS
OF GREAT MEN.

Marshal Neil's last words were: "*L'armee Francaise!*" (The French army.)
—Exchange.

What a sad thing it is to see a man close a grand career with a plagiarism in his mouth. Napoleon's last words were, "*Tete d'armee.*" (Head of the army.) Neither of those remarks amounts to anything as "last words," and reflect little credit upon the utterers. A distinguished man should be as particular about his last words as he is about his last breath. He should write them out on a slip of paper and take the judgment of his friends on them. He should never leave such a thing to the last hour of his life, and trust to an intellectual spurt at the last moment to enable him to say something smart with his latest gasp and launch into eternity with grandeur.

No—a man is apt to be too much fagged and exhausted, both in body and mind, at such a time, to be reliable; and may be the very thing he wants to say, he cannot think of to save him; and besides, there are his weeping friends bothering around; and worse than all, as likely as not he is not expecting to. A man cannot always expect to think of a natty thing to say under such circumstances, and so it is pure egotistic ostentation to put it off. There is hardly a case on record where a man came to his last moment unprepared and said a good thing—hardly a case where a man trusted to that last moment and did not make a solemn botch of it and go out of the world feeling absurd.

Now there was Daniel Webster. Nobody could tell *him* anything. *He* was not afraid. He could do something neat when the time came. And how did it turn out? Why, his will had to be fixed over; and then all his relations came; and first one thing and then another interfered, till at last he only had a chance to say "I still live," and up he went. Of course, he didn't still live, because he died—and so he might as well have kept his last words to himself as to have gone and made such a failure of it as that. A week before that, fifteen minutes of calm reflection would have enabled that man to contrive some last words that would have been a credit to himself and a comfort to his family for generations to come.

And there was John Quincy Adams. Relying on his splendid abilities and his coolness in emergencies, *he* trusted to a happy hit at the last moment to carry him through, and what was the result? Death smote him in the House of Representatives, and he observed, casually, "This is the last of earth." The last of earth! Why the "last of earth," when there was so much more left? If he had said it was the last rose of summer, or the last run of shad, it would have had just as much point to it. What he meant to say, was, "Adam was the first and Adams is the last of earth," but he put it off a trifle too long, and so he had to go with that unmeaning observation on his lips.

And there we have Napoleon? *Tete d'armee.* That don't mean anything. Taken by itself, "Head of the army" is no more important than "Head of police." And yet that was a man who could have said a good thing if he had barred out the doctor and studied over it a while. And this Marshal Neil, with half a century at his disposal, could not dash off anything better, in his last moments, than a poor plagiarism of another man's last words which were not worth plagiarizing in the first place. "The French army!" Perfectly irrelevant—perfectly flat—utterly pointless. But if he had closed one eye significantly and said, "The subscriber has made it *lively* for the French army," and then thrown a little of the comic into his last gasp, it would have been a thing to remember with satisfaction all the rest of his life. I do wish our great men would quit saying these flat things just at the moment they die. Let us have their next-to-their-last words for a while, and see if we cannot patch up something from them that will be a little more satisfactory. The public does not wish to be outraged in this way all the time.

But when we come to call to mind the last words of parties who took the trouble to make proper preparation for the occasion, we immediately notice a happy difference in the result.

There was Chesterfield. Lord Chesterfield had labored all his life to build up the most shining reputation for affability and elegance of speech and manners the world has ever seen. And could you suppose he failed to appreciate the efficiency of characteristic "last words" in the matter of seizing the successfully driven nail of such a reputation and clinching it on the other side for ever? Not he. He prepared himself. He kept his eye on the clock and his finger on his pulse. He awaited his chance. And at last, when he knew his time was come, he pretended to think a new visitor had entered, and so, with the rattle in his throat emphasized for dramatic effect, he said to the servant, "Shin around John, and get the gentleman a chair." And then he died, amid thunders of applause.

Next we have Benjamin Franklin. Franklin the author of Poor Richard's quaint sayings; Franklin the immortal axiom-builder, who used to sit up nights reducing the rankest old threadbare platitudes to crisp and snappy maxims that had a nice, varnished, original look in their new regimentals; who said, "Virtue is its own reward;" who said "Procrastination is the thief of time;" good old Franklin, the Josh Billings of the eighteenth century—though sooth to say, the latter transcends him in proverbial originality as much as he falls short of him in correctness of orthography. What sort of tactics did Franklin pursue? He pondered over his last words for as much as two weeks, and then when the time came he said "None but the brave deserve the fair," and died happy. He could not have said a sweeter thing had he lived till he was an idiot.

Byron made a poor business of it, and could not think of anything to say, at the last moment, but "Augusta—sister—Lady Byron—tell Harriet Beecher Stowe"—etc., etc.—but Shakespeare was ready and said, "England expects every man to do his duty" and went off with splendid éclat.

And there are other instances of sagacious preparation for a felicitous closing remark. For instance:

Joan of Arc said—"Tramp, tramp, tramp, the boys are marching."

Alexander the Great said—"Another of those Santa Cruz punches, if you please."

The Empress Josephine said—"Not for Jo——" and could get no further.

Cleopatra said—"The Old Guard dies, but never surrenders!"

Sir Walter Raleigh said—"Executioner, can I take your whetstone a moment, please?"

John Smith said—"Alas, I am the last of my race!"

Queen Elizabeth said—"Oh, I would give my kingdom for one moment more—I have forgotten my last words."

And Red Jacket, the noblest Indian brave that ever wielded tomahawk in deference of a friendless and persecuted race, expired with these touching words upon his lips: "*Wawkawampanoosuc, winnebagowallawallasagamore-saskatchewan.*" There was not a dry eye in the wigwam.

Let not this lesson be lost upon our public men. Let them take a healthy moment for preparation, and contrive some last words that shall be neat and to the point. Let Louis Napoleon say:

"I am content to follow my uncle, still—I do not desire to improve on his last words. Put me down for '*tete d-armee.*'"

And Garret Davis: "Let me recite the unabridged dictionary."

And H.G.: "I desire now, to say a few words on political economy."

And Mr. Bergh: "Only take part of me at a time if the load will be fatiguing to the hearse-horses."

And Andrew Johnson: "I have been an alderman, member of Congress, Governor, Senator, Pres—adieu, you know the rest."

And Seward: "Alas!—ka."

And Grant: "O."

All of which is respectfully submitted, with the most honorable intentions.

MARK TWAIN.

P.S.—I am obligated to leave out the illustrations, this time. The artist finds it impossible to make pictures of people's last words.

*L*ESS THAN A MONTH ON THE JOB AT THE *EXPRESS*, TWAIN WROTE HIS fiancée, Olivia, that items from his "People and Things" column were proving to be "excellent, as texts to string out a sketch from."[1] The next day, after routinely scrutinizing newspaper exchanges, Twain included, as one of the twenty-eight briefs in his column, this tidbit on last words: "There has been some dispute as to the last words which Lamartine uttered on his death-bed. The last version is, that the poet, a few moments previous to his death, said: 'Do not disturb me!' Marshal Neil's were '*L'armée française!*' (the French army)."

This brief indeed served as a seed from which an *Express* story germinated. On September 11, Twain published his fourth Saturday feature tale, "The Last Words of Great Men," duplicating the Neil quote as the story's inscription. His whimsical approach to the topic quickly drew the disapproval of his moral mentor, Mary Fairbanks. In response to her scolding letter, Twain sheepishly apologized for his seeming disrespect to deathbed celebrities: "Well, I'll let Death alone. I will, mother—honest—I won't bother him if he don't bother me. No, but really. I will be more reverential, if you want me to."[2]

Two days before writing Fairbanks, though, Twain could not resist milking the "taboo" subject for all it was worth. A silly ditty headlined "Personal" above his September 25 "People and Things" column facetiously reacts to "The Last Words of Great Men," is addressed to "Mr. Twain," and is signed "Yours truly, Some of the Little Women." The poem closes with "A man with a wife never *has a last word.*" Twain then adds "S'cat!" and his initials "M.T."

In the story, Twain satirically proposes that we prepare our last words ahead of time, because the public deserves thoughtful "next-to-last" words rather than rushed, nonsensical parting shots. He then surveys purported final words of some notable people before inventing a few for other well-known figures (living and dead) throughout history. Despite the story's chauvinistic title, he creates last words for Cleopatra, Joan of Arc, Napoleon I's wife, and Queen Elizabeth, as well as for a slew of great men.

There is also a comical topical reference to a controversy that occurred that fall involving Harriet Beecher Stowe and Lord and Lady Byron (a tabloid-like scandal that Twain soon exploits more fully in subsequent *Express* stories).

Forty years later, as Twain lay dying, he apparently forgot his own advice about the need to jot down memorable last comments well in advance of one's closing breaths. Newspapers at the time of his death in 1910, during his seventy-fifth year, claim his last words were, "Give me my glasses." However, scholars suggest that Twain gasped to his daughter Clara something like, "Goodbye, if we meet . . ."[3]

"The Last Words of Great Men" broke Twain's streak of illustrated *Express* Saturday features. This time, his colleague John Harrison Mills did not accompany the story with a drawing. Twain explains this absence in an amusing postscript: that he was "obligated to leave out the illustrations, this time," as his staff artist "finds it impossible to make pictures of people's last words."

Well over one hundred years later, however, Tom Toles had no problem graphically interpreting "The Last Words of Great Men" with four illustrations: Napoleon upside down, one foot still in his horse's stirrup, sword drawn (figure 4.1); Queen Elizabeth coming up empty in her closing moment (figure 4.2); Sir Walter Raleigh politely urging his executioner to pause briefly (figure 4.3); and a reclining Secretary of State William H. Seward spouting a political pun (figure 4.4).

FIGURE 4.1. Napoleon's last words; illustration by Tom Toles for Twain's *Buffalo Express* story "The Last Words of Great Men." *Image from* Buffalo Courier-Express Sunday *magazine, October 8, 1978. Courtesy of Buffalo State University Archives,* Courier-Express *Collection*

FIGURE 4.2. Queen Elizabeth's last words; illustration by Tom Toles for Twain's *Buffalo Express* story "The Last Words of Great Men." *Image from* Buffalo Courier-Express Sunday *magazine, October 8, 1978. Courtesy of Buffalo State University Archives,* Courier-Express Collection

FIGURE 4.3. Sir Walter Raleigh's last words; illustration by Tom Toles for Twain's *Buffalo Express* story "The Last Words of Great Men." *Image from* Buffalo Courier-Express Sunday *magazine, October 8, 1978. Courtesy of Buffalo State University Archives,* Courier-Express Collection

FIGURE 4.4. William Seward's last words; illustration by Tom Toles for Twain's *Buffalo Express* story "The Last Words of Great Men." *Image from* Buffalo Courier-Express Sunday *magazine, October 8, 1978. Courtesy of Buffalo State University Archives,* Courier-Express *Collection*

CHAPTER FIVE

MONSTER MASH

Twain's Exclusive Interview

"*T*he 'Wild Man.'—'Interviewed,'" yet another September 1869 Saturday feature, shows Twain again wielding his satirical sword at sensational journalism as it exploded that month with the international scandal surrounding Harriet Beecher Stowe's shocking exposé on the British poet Lord Byron. The story is presented, with commentary and the only accompanying image—a drawing in the Express by John Harrison Mills.*

Buffalo Express

SEPTEMBER 18, 1869

THE "WILD MAN."
"INTERVIEWED."

There has been so much talk about the mysterious "wild man" out there in the West for some time, that I finally felt that it was my duty to go out and "interview" him. There was something peculiarly and touchingly romantic about the creature and his strange actions, according to the newspaper reports. He was represented as being hairy, long-armed, and of great strength and stature; ugly and cumbrous; avoiding men, but appearing suddenly and unexpectedly to women and children; going armed with a club, but never molesting any creature, except sheep or other prey; fond of eating and drinking, and not particular about the quality, quantity or character of the beverages and edibles; living in the woods like a wild beast; seeming oppressed and melancholy, but never angry; moaning, and sometimes howling, but never uttering articulate sounds. Such was "Old Shep" as the papers painted him. I felt that the story of his life must be a sad one—a story of man's inhumanity to man in some shape or other—and I longed to persuade the secret from him.

"Since you say you are a member of the press," said the wild man, "I am willing to tell you all you wish to know. Bye and bye you will comprehend why it is that I am so ready to unbosom myself to a newspaper man when I have so studiously avoided conversation with other people. I will now unfold my strange story. I was born with the world we live upon, almost. I am the son of Cain."

"What!"

"I was present when the flood was announced."

"Which!"

"I am the father of the Wandering Jew."

"Sir!"

I moved out of reach of his club, and went on taking notes, but keeping a wary eye on him the while. He smiled a melancholy smile, and resumed:

"When I glance back over the dreary waste of ages, I see many a glimmering land mark that is familiar to my memory. And oh, the leagues I have traveled! the things I have seen! the events I have helped to emphasize! I was at the assassination of Caesar. I marched upon Mecca with Mahomet. I was in the Crusades, and stood with Godfrey when he planted the banner of the cross upon the battlements of Jerusalem. I ——— "

"One moment, please—have you given these items to any other journal? Can I ——— ?"

"Silence. I was in the Pinta's shrouds with Columbus when America burst upon his vision. I saw Charles I beheaded. I was in London when the Gunpowder Plot was discovered. I was present at the trial of Warren Hastings. I was on American soil when Lexington was fought—when the Declaration was promulgated—when Cornwallis surrendered—when Washington died. I entered Paris with Napoleon after Elba. I was present when you mounted your guns and manned your fleets for your war of 1812—when the South fired upon Sumter—when Richmond fell—when the President's life was taken. In all the ages, I have helped to celebrate the triumphs of genius, the achievements of arms, the havoc of storm, fire, pestilence and famine."

"Your career has been a stirring one. Might I ask how you came to locate in these dull Kansas woods, when you have been so accustomed to excitement during what I may term such a protracted period, not to put too fine a point upon it?"

"Listen. Once I was the honored servitor of the noble and illustrious" (here he heaved a sigh and passed his hairy hand across his eyes), "but in these degenerate days I am become the slave of quack doctors and newspapers. I am driven from pillar to post and hurried up and down, sometimes with stencil-plate and paste-brush to defile fences with cabalistic legends, and sometimes in grotesque and extravagant character for the behest of some driving journal. I attended to that Ocean Bank robbery some weeks ago, when I was hardly rested from finishing up the pow-wow about the completion of the Pacific Railroad; immediately I was spirited off to do an atrocious murder for the New York papers; next to attend the wedding of a patriarchal millionaire; next to raise a hurrah about the great boat race; and then, just when I had begun to hope that my old bones were to have a rest, I am bundled off to this howling wilderness to strip, and jibber, and be ugly and hairy, and pull down fences, and waylay sheep, and scare women and children, and waltz around with a club and play 'Wild Man' generally—and all to gratify the whim of a bedlam of crazy newspaper scribblers? From one end of this continent to the other, I am described as a gorilla, with a sort of human seeming about me—and all to gratify this quill-driving scum of the earth!"

"Poor old carpet-bagger!"

"I have been served infamously, often, in modern and semi-modern times. I have been compelled by base men to create fraudulent history and personate all sorts of impossible humbugs. I wrote those crazy Junius Letters; I moped in a French dungeon for fifteen years, and wore a ridiculous Iron Mask; I poked around your Northern forests, among your vagabond Indians, a solemn French idiot, personating the ghost of the dead Dauphin, that the gaping world might wonder if we had 'a Bourbon among us;' I have played sea-serpent off Nahant, and Wooly-Horse and What-is-It for the museum; I have 'interviewed' politicians for the *Sun*, worked all manner of miracles for the *Herald*, ciphered up election returns for the *World*, and thundered Political Economy through the *Tribune*. I have done all the extravagant things that the wildest invention could contrive, and done them well, and *this* is my reward—playing Wild Man in Kansas without a shirt!"

"Mysterious being, a light dawns vaguely upon me—it grows apace—what—what is your name?"

"SENSATION!"

"Hence, horrible shape!"

It spoke again:

"Oh, pitiless fate, my destiny hounds me once more. I am called. I go. Alas, is there no rest for me?"

In a moment the Wild Man's features began to soften and refine, and his form to resume a more human grace and symmetry. His club changed to a spade, and he shouldered it and started away, sighing profoundly, and shedding tears.

"Whither, poor shade?"

"TO DIG UP THE BYRON FAMILY!"

Such was the response that floated back upon the wind as the sad spirit shook its ringlets to the breeze, flourished its shovel aloft, and disappeared beyond the brow of the hill.

All of which is in strict accordance with the facts.

[L.S.]   Attest: **MARK TWAIN.**

*A*s soon as the September 1869 *Atlantic Monthly* broke Harriet Beecher Stowe's charge that the famous British poet Lord Byron had committed incest with his half-sister—Augusta Leigh— producing "an unfortunate child of sin," newspapers on both sides of the pond had a field day.[1] So did Mark Twain.

Like a dog with a bone, Twain latched on to the "Byron Scandal" and didn't let go. From August 1869 to January 1870, he filled the pages of the *Buffalo Express* with commentary on the controversy. In the process, he continued to condemn sensationalized journalism and mostly defend Stowe from widespread accusations of libel.

Twain alludes to the Byron Scandal seven times in his "People and Things" snippets[2] and in seven full-fledged editorials. He also spoofs it in three of his front-page Saturday features (as we have already seen in "The Last Words of Great Men"). The Byron dustup is most prominent in the Saturday feature of September 18, "The 'Wild Man.' 'Interviewed.'"

In this fable, intrepid reporter Mark Twain tracks down a legendary protean monster who has been in hiding from packs of journalists. The "Wild Man" has witnessed every significant and tawdry global event throughout the ages, from Caesar's assassination to notorious murders and weddings to American Civil War catastrophes. Throughout history, the "crazy newspaper scribbler" and "quill-driving scum" fraternity has delighted in twisting his eyewitness accounts into juicy, fraudulent versions of the truth.

Twain locates the "Wild Man" in Kansas and scores an exclusive one-on-one "scoop." The interview with the monster again reveals Twain's own distaste with the current trend he sees toward sensational, distorted newspaper reporting designed to meet the prurient needs of readers.

As the interview closes, Twain coaxes the "Wild Man" to identify himself as "Sensation" and admit that the next stop on his legendary itinerary is to quench the public's thirst for more salacious tidbits on the Byron matter.

During the raging Byron Scandal, Twain may have let Harriet Beecher Stowe off lightly because his future in-laws, the Langdons, were close to the Beecher clan. As fate would have it, five years later when Twain built a house in Hartford, Connecticut, Harriet Beecher Stowe was his next-door neighbor.

"The 'Wild Man.' 'Interviewed'" was Twain's last Saturday *Express* feature story illustrated by John Harrison Mills. The drawing depicts Twain seated with pad and pencil taking notes, just before the monster's cudgel turns into a shovel to dig up more Byron-related dirt (figure 5.1).

prom," said the wild man, "I am willing to | "To dig up the Byron family !"

FIGURE 5.1. "To Dig Up the Byron Family!" This John Harrison Mills illustration accompanied Twain's *Buffalo Express* story "The 'Wild Man.' 'Interviewed.'" *Image from the* Buffalo Express, *September 18, 1869*

CHAPTER SIX

THE TAX MAN COMETH

Twain's Cagey Caller

---

*A*s a newlywed in 1870, Twain mostly wrote at home rather than at the Express office, and some of his comic features took on a domestic flavor. The first of these was "A Mysterious Visit," in which the Twain-inspired idiot narrator is entirely too chatty with a visitor, who turns out to be an IRS agent. The story is presented, followed by commentary, an illustration by True Williams from the 1875 Sketches, New and Old, and two drawings by Tom Toles from a 1978 edition of the Buffalo Courier-Express Sunday *magazine.*

𝕭𝖚𝖋𝖋𝖆𝖑𝖔 𝕰𝖝𝖕𝖗𝖊𝖘𝖘

MARCH 19, 1870

[FROM MARK TWAIN.]
A MYSTERIOUS VISIT.

The first notice that was taken of me when I first "settled down" recently, was by a gentleman who said he was an assessor, and connected with the U.S. Internal Revenue Department. I said I had never heard of his branch of business before, but was very glad to see him, all the same—would he sit down? He sat down. I did not know anything particular to say, and yet felt that people who have arrived at the particular dignity of keeping house must be conversational, must be easy and sociable in company. So in default of anything else to say, I asked him if he was opening his shop in our neighborhood.

He said he was. (I did not wish to appear ignorant, but I had hoped he would mention what he had for sale.)

I ventured to ask him "how was trade?" and he said "so-so."

I then said we would drop in, and if we liked his house as well as any other, we would give him our custom.

He said we would like his establishment well enough to confine ourselves to it—said he never saw anyone who would go off and hunt up another man in his line after trading with him once.

That sounded pretty complacent, but barring that natural expression of villainy which we all have, the man looked honest enough.

I do not know how it came about, exactly, but gradually we appeared to melt down and run together, conversationally speaking, and then everything went along as comfortably as clockwork.

We talked, and talked, and talked—at least I did. And we laughed, and laughed, and laughed—at least he did. But all the time, I had my presence of mind about me—I had my native shrewdness turned on, "full head," as the engineers say. I was determined to find out all about his business, in spite of his obscure answers—and I was determined I would have it out of him without his suspecting what I was at. I meant to trap him with a deep, deep ruse. I would tell him about my own business, and he would naturally so warm to me during this seductive burst of confidence that he would forget himself and tell me all about his affairs before he suspected what I was about. I thought to myself, My son, you little know what an old fox you are dealing with. I said:

"Now you would never guess what I made lecturing, this winter and this spring."

"No—I don't believe I could, to save me. Let me see—let me see. About two thousand dollars maybe? But no—no, sir. I know you couldn't have made that much. Say seventeen hundred, maybe?"

"Ha-Ha—I knew you couldn't. My lecturing receipts for last spring and this winter were fourteen thousand, seven hundred and fifty dollars. What do you think of that?"

"Why, it is amazing—perfectly amazing. I will make a note of it. And you say even that wasn't all?"

"All? Why bless you there was my income from the Buffalo Express for four months—about—about—well, what would you say to about eight thousand dollars, for instance?"

"Say! Why I should say I should like to see myself rolling in just such an ocean of affluence. Eight thousand! I'll make a note of it. Why, man—and on top of this I am to understand that you have still more income?"

"Ha-ha-ha! Why, you're only in the suburbs of it, so to speak. There's my book, "The Innocents Abroad"—price $3.50 to $5.00, according to the binding. Listen to me. Look me in the eye. During the last four months and a half, saying nothing of sale before that,—but just simply during the four months and a half ending March 15, 1870, we've sold ninety-five thousand copies of that book! Ninety-five thousand! Think of it. An average four dollars a copy, say. It's nearly four hundred thousand dollars, my son. I get half."

"The suffering Moses! I'll set *that* down. Fourteen-seven-fifty—eight—two hundred. Total, say—well, upon my word, the grand total is about two hundred and thirteen thousand dollars. *Is* that possible?"

"Possible! If there's any mistake it's the other way. Two hundred and fourteen thousand, cash, is my income for this year if *I* know how to cipher."

Then the gentleman got up to go. It came over me most uncomfortably that maybe I had made my revelations for nothing, besides being flattered into stretching them considerably by the stranger's astonished exclamations. But no; at the last moment the gentleman handed me a large envelope and said it contained his advertisement; and that I would find out all about his business in it; and that he would be happy to have my custom—would in fact be proud to have the custom of a man of such prodigious income; and that he used to think there were several wealthy men in Buffalo, but when they came to trade with him he discovered that they had barely enough to live on; and that in truth it had been such a weary, weary age since he had seen a rich man face to face, and talked with him, and touched him with his hands, that he could hardly refrain from embracing me—in fact, would esteem it a great favor if I would *let* him embrace me.

This so pleased me that I did not try to resist, but allowed this simple hearted stranger to throw his arms about me and weep a few tranquilizing tears down the back of my neck. Then he went his way.

As soon as he was gone, I opened his advertisement. I studied it attentively for four minutes. I then called up the cook and said:

"Hold me while I faint. Let Maria turn the batter-cakes."

By and bye, when I came to, I sent down to the rum mill on the corner and hired an artist by the week to sit up nights and curse that stranger, and give me a lift occasionally in the day time when I came to a hard place.

Ah, what a miscreant he was! His "advertisement" was nothing in the world but a wicked tax return—a string of impertinent questions about my private affairs occupying the best part of four foolscap pages of fine print—questions, I may remark, gotten up with such marvelous ingenuity that the oldest man in the world couldn't understand what the most of them were driving at—questions, too, that were calculated to make a man report about four times his actual income to keep from swearing to a lie. I looked for loopholes, but there did not appear to be any. Inquiry No. 1 covered my case, as generously and as amply as an umbrella could cover an ant hill.

"What were your profits, in 1869, from any trade, business, or vocation, wherever carried out?"

And that inquiry was backed up by thirteen others of an equally searching nature, the most modest of which required information as to whether I had committed any burglary, or highway robbery, or by any arson or other secret source of emolument had acquired property which was not enumerated in my statement of income as set opposite to Inquiry No. 1.

It was plain that that stranger had enabled me to make an ass of myself. It was very, very plain and I went out and hired another artist. By working on my vanity the stranger had induced me into declaring an income of $214,000. By law, $1,000 of this was exempt from income tax—the only relief I could see, and it was only a drop in the ocean. At the legal five per cent, I must pay over to the government the appalling sum of ten thousand six hundred and fifty dollars, income tax.

(I may remark, in this place, that I did not do it.)

I am acquainted with a very opulent man, whose house is a palace, whose table is regal, whose outlays are enormous. Yet a man who has no income, as I have often noticed, by the revenue returns; and to him I went for advice, in my distress. He took my dreadful exhibition of receipts, he put on his glasses, he took his pen, and presto!—I was a pauper! It was the neatest thing that ever was. He did it simply by deftly manipulating the bill of "deductions." He set down my "state, national, and municipal taxes" as so much; my "losses by shipwreck, fire, etc.," at so much; my "losses on sale of real estate"—on "livestock sold"— on "payments for rent of homestead"—on "repairs, improvement, interest"—on "previously taxed salary as an officer of the United States army, navy, revenue service," and other things. He got astonishing "deductions" out of each and every one of these matters—each and every one of them.

And when he was done he handed me the paper and I saw at a glance that during the year of 1869 my income, in the way of profits, had been *one thousand two hundred and fifty dollars and forty cents.*

"Now," said he, "the thousand dollars is exempt by law. What you want to do is go and swear this document in and pay tax on the two hundred and fifty dollars."

(While he was making this speech his little boy Willie lifted a two dollar greenback out of his vest pocket and vanished with it, and I would bet anything that if my stranger were to call on that little boy tomorrow he would make a false return of his income.)

"Do you," said I, "do you always work up the 'deductions' after this fashion in your own case, sir?"

"Well, I should say so! If it weren't for these eleven saving clauses under the head of 'Deductions' I should be beggared every year to support this hateful and wicked, this extortionate and tyrannical government."

This gentleman stands away up among the very best of the solid men of Buffalo—the men of moral weight, of commercial integrity, of unimpeachable social spotlessness—and so I bowed to his example. I went down to the revenue office, and under the accusing eyes of my old visitor I stood up and swore to lie after lie, fraud after fraud, villainy after villainy, till my immortal soul was covered inches and inches thick with perjury and my self respect was gone forever and ever.

But what of it? It is nothing more than thousands of the highest, and richest, and proudest, and most respected, honored, and courted men in America do every year. And so I don't care. I am not ashamed.

I shall simply, for the present, talk little and wear fireproof gloves, lest I fall into certain habits irrevocably.

MARK TWAIN

*A*FTER TWAIN TOOK A FOUR-MONTH HIATUS FROM HIS OFFICE WORK at the *Buffalo Express* to lecture and to get married, he and his new bride established residence in a splendid wedding-gift mansion on Buffalo's most prestigious boulevard, Delaware Street, in February 1870. Almost immediately as a new homeowner, he welcomed all manner of callers. One was a door-to-door lightning rod salesman, whose visit Twain quickly fashioned into a humorous fictional account for the *Galaxy* magazine. Another early visitor was an Internal Revenue Service collector.

A few weeks after Twain's marriage, newspapers reported that Twain was likely to make $100,000 in royalties from the sales of *The Innocents Abroad*. Shortly thereafter, the IRS sent a letter inquiring about his tax bill—which would amount to 5 percent of his gross income over $1,000. Soon a collector dropped off a form with several questions pertaining to Twain's income. Twain had a difficult time answering the questions, as deletions—changes made in pencil and in two colors of ink—suggest.

Twain apparently found the IRS assessor's visit and his own bookkeeping struggles amusing enough to once again adopt his Mark Twain-as-inspired-idiot persona and craft another comic tall tale, "A Mysterious Visit." The column was published in the March 19, 1870, issue of the *Buffalo Express*.

In it, the unsuspecting narrator is tricked by his wily visitor into blathering on and on about his more-than-comfortable financial status. Unwittingly, he is bragging to an IRS agent, who eagerly records the inflated earnings from the *Buffalo Express* and exaggerated royalties from *The Innocents Abroad* supplied by Twain.

The kicker is when the Twain narrator consults his mega-rich neighbor (perhaps his next-door neighbor, real estate magnate James S. Lyon, whose mansion dwarfed Twain's own) for advice in the aftermath of the disastrous disclosure.

As a new member of the Delaware Street nouveau riche, Twain benefits from the tips of his fellow member of Buffalo's upper crust on how to find tax deductions and loopholes, so that in the end, the $214,000 income that Twain had boasted of to the IRS agent is whittled down to a measly $250.14.

At one point in "A Mysterious Visit," the garrulous narrator writes, "And we laughed, and laughed, and laughed—at least he did." Turns out, the federal tax collectors really did have a sense of humor. An entire page of the Saturday, April 9, 1870, *Internal Revenue Record* is devoted to a reprint of Twain's comic story. It had been submitted by the assistant assessors in the Thirtieth District (Buffalo), because it was "suggestive of some fun."[1]

Twain reprised the story in his 1875 collection, *Sketches, New and Old*, again with a rendering by artist True Williams (figure 6.1).

When "A Mysterious Visit" was reprinted 108 years later, in the *Sunday* magazine of the May 7, 1978, *Buffalo Courier-Express*, staff illustrator Tom Toles provided two accompanying drawings.

The first shows the unsuspecting Twain welcoming into his home an affable-looking, hat-doffing gentleman carrying a briefcase (figure 6.2). (Another lightning rod salesman, perhaps?)

FIGURE 6.1. Twain narrator talking with visitor; illustration by True Williams for Twain's *Buffalo Express* story "A Mysterious Visit." *Image from* Mark Twain's Sketches, New and Old *(Hartford, CT: American Publishing Company, 1875), 316*

Illustrations by TOM TOLES

FIGURE 6.2. Twain narrator welcoming visitor; illustration by Tom Toles for Twain's *Buffalo Express* story "A Mysterious Visit." *Image from the* Buffalo Courier-Express Sunday *magazine, May 7, 1978. Courtesy of Buffalo State University Archives,* Courier-Express *Collection*

The second drawing depicts Twain in the parlor with his visitor, comfortably chatting up his newly acquired wealth (figure 6.3).

Ironically, during the miserable closing weeks of his residency in Buffalo—one year after "A Mysterious Visit" appeared—Twain did indeed have real tax woes. In early March 1871, he once again had trouble filling out his federal income tax worksheet—this time for 1870 earnings. And just days before he, Olivia, and their ailing infant son moved from Buffalo to Elmira, New York, a distraught Twain ranted about the "ruinous" local tax structure in western New York.

FIGURE 6.3. Twain narrator and visitor in conversation; illustration by Tom Toles for Twain's *Buffalo Express* story "A Mysterious Visit." *Image from the* Buffalo Courier-Express Sunday *magazine, May 7, 1978. Courtesy of Buffalo State University Archives,* Courier-Express *Collection*

CHAPTER SEVEN

DYING TO GET IN, DYING TO GET OUT

Twain and Cemetery Reform

---

*T*wain's *"Curious Dream" represented another domicile-based plot, but with a dash of social reform and reverie. It's about a decaying graveyard in his tony Buffalo neighborhood. The story was published in the* Buffalo Express *in two parts, on the last Saturday in April and the first Saturday in May 1870. It was reprinted as a whole, titled "A Curious Dream," in* Sketches, New and Old *(1875) and featured four illustrations by True Williams. The two-part* Express *version is presented here, followed by commentary, the four artworks by Williams, and one 1983 illustration by Bill Watterson, who soon became famous for his* Calvin and Hobbes *comic strip.*

Buffalo Express

APRIL 30, 1870

[FROM MARK TWAIN.]

CURIOUS DREAM.

CONTAINING A MORAL.

Night before last I had a singular dream. I seemed to be sitting on a doorstep, (in no particular city, perhaps), ruminating, and the time of night appeared to be about twelve or one o'clock. The weather was balmy and delicious. There was no human sound in the air, not even a footstep. There was no sound of any kind to emphasize the dead stillness, except the occasional hollow barking of a dog in the distance and the fainter answer of a further dog. Presently up the street I heard a bony clack-clacking, and guessed it was the castanets of a serenading party. In a minute more a tall skeleton, hooded and half-clad in a tattered and mouldy shroud whose shreds were flapping about the ribby lattice-work of its person, swung by me with a stately stride, and disappeared in the gray gloom of the starlight. It had a broken and worm-eaten coffin on its shoulder and a bundle of something in its hand. I knew what the clack-clacking was, then—it was the party's joints working together, and his elbows knocking against his sides as he walked. I may say I was surprised. Before I could collect my thoughts and enter upon any speculations as to what this apparition might portend, I heard another one coming—for I recognized his clack-clack. He had two-thirds of a coffin on his shoulder, and some foot and head-boards under his arm. I mightily wanted to peer under his hood and speak to him, but when he turned and smiled upon me with his cavernous sockets and his projecting grin as he went by, I thought I would not detain him. He was hardly gone when I heard the clacking again, and another one issued from the shadowy half-light. This one was bending under a heavy grave stone, and dragging a shabby coffin after him by a string. When he got to me he gave me a steady look for a moment or two, and then rounded to and backed up to me, saying:

"Ease this down for a fellow, would you?"

I eased the grave-stone down till it rested on the ground, and in doing so noticed that it bore the name of "John Baxter Copmanhurst," with "May, 1839," as the date of his death. Deceased sat wearily down by me and wiped his os frontis with his major maxillary—chiefly from former habit I judged, for I could not see that he brought away any perspiration.

"It is too bad, too bad," said he, drawing the remnant of the shroud about him and leaning his jaw pensively on his hand. Then he put his left foot up on his knee and fell to scratching his ancle bone absently with a rusty nail which he got out of his coffin.

"What is too bad, friend?"

"Oh, everything, everything. I almost wish I never had died."

"You surprise me. Why do you say this? Has anything gone wrong? What is the matter?"

"Matter! Look at this shroud—rags. Look at this gravestone, all battered up. Look at that disgraceful old coffin. All a man's property going to ruin and destruction before his eyes and ask him if anything is wrong? Fire and brimstone!"

"Calm yourself, calm yourself," I said. "It *is* too bad—it is certainly too bad, but then I had not supposed that you would much mind such matters, situated as you are."

"Well, my dear sir, I *do* mind them. My pride is hurt and my comfort is impaired—destroyed, I might say. I will state my case—I will put it to you in such a way that you can comprehend it, if you will let me," said the poor skeleton, tilting the hood of his shroud back, as if he were clearing for action, and thus unconsciously giving himself a jaunty and festive air very much at variance with the grave character of his position in life—so to speak—and in prominent contrast with his distressful mood.

"Proceed," said I.

"I reside in the shameful old grave yard a block or two above you here, in this street—There, now, I just expected that cartilage would let go!—Third rib from the bottom, friend, hitch the end of it to my spine with a string, if you have got such a thing about you, though a bit of silver wire is a deal pleasanter, and more durable and becoming, if one keeps it polished—to think of shredding out and going to pieces in this way, just on account of the indifference and neglect of one's posterity!"—and the poor ghost grated his teeth in a way that gave me a wrench and a shiver—for the effect is mightily increased by the absence of muffling flesh and cuticle. "I reside in that old graveyard, and have for these thirty years; and I tell you things are changed since I first laid this tired old frame there, and turned over and stretched out for a long sleep, and with a delicious sense upon me of being done with bother, and grief, and anxiety, and doubt and fear, forever and ever, and listening with comfortable and increasing satisfaction to the sexton's work, from the startling clatter of his first spade-full on my coffin till it dulled away to the faint patting that shaped the roof of my new home—delicious? My! I wish you could try it to-night!" and out of my reverie deceased fetched me with a rattling slap with a bony hand.

"Yes, sir, thirty years ago I laid me down there, and was happy. For it was out in the country, then—out in the breezy, flowery, grand old woods, and the lazy winds gossiped with the leaves, and the squirrels capered over us and around us, and the creeping things visited us, and the birds filled the tranquil solitude with music. Ah, it was worth ten years of a man's life to be dead then! Every thing was pleasant. I was in a good neighborhood, for all the dead people that lived near me belonged to the best families in the city. Our posterity appeared to think the world of us. They kept our graves in the very best condition; the fences were always in faultless repair, headboards were kept painted or whitewashed, and were replaced with new ones as soon as they began to look rusty or decayed; monuments were kept upright, railings intact and bright, the rosebushes and shrubbery trimmed, trained and free from blemish, the walks clean and smooth and graveled. But that day is gone by. Our descendants have forgotten us. My grandson lives in a stately house built with money made by these old hands of mine, and I sleep in a neglected grave with invading vermin that gnaw my shroud to build them nests withal! I and friends that lie with me founded and secured the prosperity of this fine city, and the stately bantling of our loves leaves us to rot in a dilapidated cemetery which neighbors curse and strangers scoff at. See the difference between the old time and this—for instance: Our graves are all caved in, now; our head-boards have rotted away and tumbled down; our railings reel this way and that, with one foot in the air, after a fashion of unseemly levity; our monuments lean wearily and our gravestones bow their heads discouraged; there be no adornments any more,—no roses, nor shrubs, nor graveled walks, nor anything that is a comfort to the eye, and even the paintless old board fence that did make a show of holding us sacred from companionship with beasts and the defilement of heedless feet, has tottered till it overhangs the street, and only advertises the presence of our dismal resting place and invites yet more derision to it. And now we cannot hide our poverty and tatters in the friendly woods, for the city has stretched its withering arms abroad and taken us in, and all that remains of the cheer of our old home is the cluster of lugubrious forest trees that stand, bored and weary of city life, with their feet in our coffins, looking into the hazy distance and not wishing they were there. I tell you, it is disgraceful!

"You begin to comprehend—you begin to see how it is. While our descendants are living sumptuously on our money right around us in the city, we have to fight hard to keep skull and bones together. Bless you there isn't a grave in our cemetery that doesn't leak—not one. Every time it rains in the night we have to climb out and roost in the trees—and sometimes we are wakened suddenly by the chilly water trickling down the back of our necks. Then I tell you there is a general heaving up of old graves and kicking over old monuments, and scampering of old skeletons for the trees! Bless me, if you had gone along there some such nights after twelve you might have seen as many as fifteen of us roosting on one limb, with our joints rattling drearily and the wind wheezing through our ribs! Many a time we have perched there for three or four dreary hours, and then come down, stiff and chilled through and drowsy, and borrowed each other's skulls to bail out our graves with—if you will glance up in my mouth, now as I tilt my head back, you can see that my head-piece is half full of old dry sediment—how top-heavy and stupid it makes me sometimes! Yes, sir, many a time if you had happened to come along just before the dawn you'd have caught us baling out the graves and hanging our shrouds on the fence to dry. Why, I had an elegant shroud stolen from there one morning—think a party by the name of Smith took it, that resides in a plebian graveyard over yonder—I think so because the first time I ever saw him he hadn't anything on but a check shirt, and the last time I saw him, which was at a social gathering in the new cemetery, he was the best dressed corpse in the company—and it is a significant fact that he left when he saw me; and presently an old woman from here missed her coffin—she generally took it with her when she went anywhere, because she was liable to take cold and bring on the spasmodic rheumatism that originally killed her if she exposed herself to the night air much. She was named Hotchkiss—Anna Matilda Hotchkiss—you might know her? She has two upper front teeth, is tall, but a good deal inclined to stoop; one rib on the left side gone, has one shred of rusty hair hanging from the left side of her head, and one little tuft just above and a little forward of her right ear, has her under jaw wired on one side where it had worked loose, small bone of left forearm gone—lost in a fight—has a kind of swagger in her gait and a 'gallus' way of going with her arms akimbo and her nostrils in the air—has been pretty free and easy, and is all damaged and battered up till she looks like a queensquare crate in ruins—maybe you have met her?"

"God forbid!" I involuntarily ejaculated, for some how I was not looking for that form of question, and it caught me a little off my guard. But I hastened to make amends for my rudeness and say: "I simply meant I had not had the honor—for I would not deliberately speak discourteously of a friend of yours. You were saying that you were robbed—and it was a shame, too—but it appears by what is left of the shroud you have on that it was a costly one in its day. How did ——"

A most ghastly expression began to develop among the decayed features and shriveled integuments of my guest's face, and I was beginning to grow uneasy and distressed, when he told me he was only working up a deep, sly smile, with a wink in it, to suggest that about the time he acquired his present garment a ghost in a neighboring cemetery missed one. This reassured me, but I begged him to confine himself to speech, thenceforth, because his facial expression was uncertain. Even with the most elaborate care it was liable to miss fire. Smiling should especially be avoided. What *he* might honestly consider a shining success was likely to strike me in a very different light. I said I liked to see a skeleton cheerful, even decorously playful, but I did not think smiling was a skeleton's best hold.

MARK TWAIN.

[Conclusion—with the rest of the MORAL—next week.]

Buffalo Express

[FROM MARK TWAIN.]

CURIOUS DREAM.

CONTAINING A MORAL.

[CONCLUDED FROM LAST WEEK'S EXPRESS]

[In the chapter preceding this, was set forth how certain shrouded skeletons came mysteriously marching past my door after midnight, carrying battered tombstones, crumbling coffins, and such like property with them, and how one sat down by me to rest, (having also his tombstone with him, and dragging after him his worm-eaten coffin by a string.) and complained at great length of the discomforts of his ruinous and long-neglected graveyard. This conversation now continueth.]

"Yes, friend," said the poor skeleton, "the facts are just as I have given them to you. Two of these old graveyards—the one that I resided in and one further along—have been deliberately neglected by our descendants of to-day until there is no occupying them any longer. Aside from the osteological discomfort of it—and that is no light matter this rainy weather—the present state of things is ruinous to property. We have got to move or be content to see our effects wasted away and utterly destroyed. Now you will hardly believe it, but it is true, nevertheless, that there isn't a single coffin in good repair among all my acquaintance—now that is an absolute fact. I do not refer to people who come in a pine box mounted on an express wagon, but I am talking about your high-toned silver-mounted burial-case, monumental sort, that travel under plumes at the head of a procession and have choice of cemetery lots—I mean folks like the Jarvis's, and the Bledsoe's and the Burling's and such. They are all about ruined. The most substantial people in our set, they were. And now look at them—utterly used up and poverty-stricken. One of the Bledsoe's actually traded his monument to a late barkeeper for some fresh shavings to put under his head. I tell you it speaks volumes, for there is nothing a corpse takes so much pride in as his monument. He loves to read the inscription. He comes after awhile to believe what it says, himself, and then you may see him sitting on the fence night after night enjoying it. Epitaphs are cheap, and they do a poor chap a world of good after he is dead, especially if he had hard luck while he was alive. I wish

70   THE ILLUSTRATED MARK TWAIN AND THE *BUFFALO EXPRESS*

they were used more. Now I don't complain, but confidentially, I *do* think it was a little shabby in my descendants to give me nothing but this old slab of a gravestone—and all the more that there isn't a compliment on it. It used to have

"GONE TO HIS JUST REWARD"

on it, and I was proud when I first saw it, but by and bye I noticed that whenever an old friend of mine came along he would hook his chin on the railing and pull a long face and read along down till he came to that, and then he would chuckle to himself and walk off looking satisfied and comfortable. So I scratched it off to get rid of those fools. But a dead man always takes a deal of pride in his monument. Yonder goes half a dozen of Jarvises, now, with the family monument along. And Smithers and some hired spectres went by with his a while ago. Hello, Higgins, good-bye old friend! That's Meredith Higgins—died in '44— belongs to our set in the cemetery—fine old family—great-grandmother was an Injun—I am on the most familiar terms with him—he didn't hear me was the reason he didn't answer me. And I am sorry, too, because I would have liked to introduce you. You would admire him. He is the most disjointed, sway-backed and generally distorted old skeleton you ever saw, but he is full of fun. When he laughs it sounds like rasping two stones together, and he always starts it off with a cheery screech like raking a nail across a window-pane. Hey, Jones! That is old Columbus Jones—shroud cost four hundred dollars—entire trousseau, including monument, twenty-seven hundred. This was in the Spring of '26. It was enormous style for those days. Dead people came all the way from the Alleghenies to see his things—the party that occupied the grave next to mine remembers it well. Now do you see that individual going along with a piece of a headboard under his arm, one leg bone below his knee gone, and not a thing in the world on? That is Barstow Dalhouse, and next to Columbus Jones. He was the most sumptuously outfitted person that ever entered our cemetery. We are all leaving. We cannot tolerate the treatment we are receiving at the hands of our descendants. They open new cemeteries, but they leave us to our ignominy. They mend the streets, but they never mend anything that is about us or belongs to us. Look at that coffin of mine—yet I tell you in its day it was a piece of furniture that would have attracted attention in any drawing-room in the city. You may have it if you want it—I can't afford to repair it. Put a new bottom on her, and part of a new top, and a bit of fresh lining along the left side, and you'll find her about as comfortable as any receptacle of her species you ever tried. No thanks—no, don't mention it—you have been civil to me and I would give you all the property I have got before I would seem ungrateful. Now this winding-sheet is a kind of a sweet thing in its way, if you would like to ——. No? Well, just as you say, but I wished to be fair and liberal—there's nothing mean about *me*. Good-bye, friend, I must be going. I may have a good way to go to-night—don't know. I only know one thing for certain, and that is, that I am on the emigrant trail, now, and I'll never sleep in that crazy old cemetery again. I will travel till I find respectable quarters, if I have to hoof it to New Jersey. All the boys are going. It was decided in public conclave, last night, to emigrate, and by the time the sun rises there won't be a bone left in our old habitations. Such cemeteries may suit my surviving friends but they do not suit the remains that have the honor to make these remarks. My opinion is the general opinion. If you doubt it, go and see how the departing ghosts upset things before they started. They were almost riotous in their demonstrations of distaste. Hello, here are some of the Bledsoes, and if you will give me a lift with this tombstone I guess I will join company and jog along with them—mighty respectable old family, the Bledsoes, and used to always come out with six-horse hearses, and all that sort of thing fifty years ago when I walked these streets in daylight. Good-bye, friend."

And with his gravestone on his shoulder he joined the grisly procession, dragging his damaged coffin after him, for notwithstanding he pressed it upon me so earnestly, I utterly refused his hospitality. I suppose that for as much as two hours these sad outcasts went clacking by, laden with their dismal effects, and all that time I sat pitying them. One or two of the youngest and least dilapidated of them inquired about midnight trains on the railways, but the rest seemed unacquainted with that mode of travel, and merely asked about common public roads to various towns and cities, some of which are not on the map, now, and vanished from it and from the earth as much as thirty years ago, and some few of them never had existed any where but on maps, and private ones in real estate agencies at that. And they asked about the condition of the cemeteries in these towns and cities, and about the reputation the citizens bore as to reverence for the dead.

This whole matter interested me deeply, and likewise compelled my sympathy for these homeless ones. And it all seeming real, and I not knowing it was a dream, I mentioned to one shrouded wanderer an idea that had entered my head to publish an account of this curious and very sorrowful exodus, but said also that I could not describe it truthfully, and just as it occurred, without seeming to trifle with a grave subject and exhibit an irreverence for the dead that would shock and distress their surviving friends. But this bland and stately remnant of a former citizen leaned far over my gate and whispered in my ear, and said:

"DO NOT LET THAT DISTURB YOU. THE COMMUNITY THAT CAN STAND SUCH GRAVEYARDS AS THOSE WE ARE EMIGRATING FROM CAN STAND ANY THING A BODY CAN SAY ABOUT THE NEGLECTED AND FORSAKEN DEAD THAT LIE IN THEM."

At that very moment a cock crowed, and the weird procession vanished and left not a shred or a bone behind. I awoke, and found myself lying with my head out of the bed and "sagging" downwards considerably—a position favorable to dreaming dreams with morals in them, may be, but not poetry.

MARK TWAIN.

SHORTLY AFTER MOVING INTO HIS WEDDING-GIFT MANSION, TWAIN sharply curtailed his appearances at his *Buffalo Express* office. From March 1870 to March 1871, he mostly conducted business—writing and editorial, layout, and story-selection decisions—from the comfort of his up-stairs den at home. A courier delivered Twain's stories and instructions the 1.4 miles to his newspaper staff.

It is no surprise, then, that he cultivated his neighborhood for story ideas, since he seldom ventured far from his new house. A handful of *Express* stories in 1870 were inspired by people, places, and events derived from his Delaware Street district. One of them was the two-part "Curious Dream," published in the *Express* on consecutive Saturdays in late April and early May.

This macabre fantasy was likely inspired by observations while strolling his neighborhood—his favorite means of recreation. During his quick, two-and-a-half-block jaunts northward from home to church at Westminster Presbyterian, Twain would have frequently passed the old North Street cemetery and noticed its dilapidated condition.

The five-acre cemetery on the southwest corner of Delaware and North Streets, bounded on the west by Bowery Street, was founded in 1830. Its once neatly trimmed lawns, raked gravel paths, and well-maintained fences had suffered years of neglect by the time Twain arrived on the scene in February 1870. Instead, Twain saw a cemetery overgrown with weeds, tombstones in disrepair, and fences missing. The eyesore of a cemetery had become the "resort" of tramps during daylight and of "bad characters" after dark.

In his grisly yet comic satire, the Mark Twain narrator dreams of sitting on the front steps of his Delaware Street home watching frustrated skeleton after skeleton walk by, as they abandon the ruined cemetery and drag their decayed coffins behind them.

For decades thereafter, local legend held that Twain's story brought about the reform of the North Street cemetery. The story might indeed have brought fresh public attention to the cemetery's dire disrepair. However, remedial action had been underway for some years. Already in 1867, the new property owner had begun removing bodies for reinterment in the more prestigious Forest Lawn Cemetery. This process peaked in 1871 when fifty bodies were removed.[1]

By 1886, the old North Street cemetery was fully evacuated, and the valuable real estate was ripe for private developers. Indeed, charming houses soon sprouted on Bowery Street, renamed Irving Place. As a youngster, in 1898, F. Scott Fitzgerald lived with his family in a luxury hotel built on the site of the old cemetery, and five years later in a lovely home on Irving Place.

"Curious Dream" begins when the Twain narrator's peaceful midnight reverie on his front steps is disturbed by a ghoulish parade of corpses as they flee the ruined North Street cemetery with their "belongings" in disgust. One of them, John Baxter Copmanhurst, who claims to have been a resident since 1839, pauses to air his grievances to the narrator. Copmanhurst reminisces about the longstanding prestige of burial at North Street cemetery, that all the dead people buried near him "belonged to the best families of Buffalo" and that it was a "good neighborhood." Then the cemetery was neglected and allowed to rot.

So the residents convened a meeting and decided to leave the run-down premises, hoisting their decayed, broken coffins over their shoulders or pulling them with ropes. Copmanhurst's expensive coffin alone was in its day "a piece of furniture that would have attracted attention in any drawing room in the city." He further complains that while he and his fellow deceased city pioneers lie in eternal discomfort, their living relatives luxuriate with inherited fortunes.

The narrator continues to sit into the wee hours watching the "grisly procession," giving advice on train schedules and recommending well-maintained alternative local cemetery sites.

Once the narrator awakens from his dream, he vows to tell the tale of how these former distinguished Buffalo citizens were disrespected in death.

For his illustrations of "Curious Dream" for *Mark Twain's Sketches, New and Old* in 1875, artist True Williams drew Twain on his front steps chatting with Copmanhurst (figure 7.1); the wrecked state of North Street cemetery, with busted-up fences, tall grass and weeds, and tipped gravestones (figure 7.2); a corpse on the run in the moonlight (figure 7.3); and Twain about to wake from his nightmare, perhaps induced by the awkward position of his head (figure 7.4).

FIGURE 7.1. Twain narrator listening to skeleton's complaint; illustration by True Williams for Twain's *Buffalo Express* two-part story "Curious Dream." *Image from* Mark Twain's Sketches, New and Old *(Hartford, CT: American Publishing Company, 1875), 192*

FIGURE 7.2. Dilapidated condition of neighborhood cemetery; illustration by True Williams for Twain's two-part *Buffalo Express* story "Curious Dream." *Image from* Mark Twain's Sketches, New and Old *(Hartford, CT: American Publishing Company, 1875), 195*

FIGURE 7.3. Skeleton fleeing rundown cemetery; illustration by True Williams for Twain's two-part *Buffalo Express* story "Curious Dream." *Image from* Mark Twain's Sketches, New and Old *(Hartford, CT: American Publishing Company, 1875), 197*

FIGURE 7.4. Narrator asleep in awkward, dream-inducing position; illustration by True Williams for Twain's two-part *Buffalo Express* story "Curious Dream." *Image from* Mark Twain's Sketches, New and Old *(Hartford, CT: American Publishing Company, 1875), 201*

More than one hundred years later, in 1983, cartoonist Bill Watterson depicted the overall scenario of Twain in front of his porch at night talking with one fleeing corpse while others pass by in the background (figure 7.5).

FIGURE 7.5. Twain narrator amid skeletons abandoning neighborhood cemetery; 1983 illustration by Bill Watterson for Twain's two-part *Buffalo Express* story "Curious Dream." *Image courtesy of Irene Wong, Mark Twain Journal*

CHAPTER EIGHT

WHY DID THE CHICKEN CROSS THE ROAD?

To Get "Raised" by Twain

*M*ark Twain drew on a beloved animal-loving neighbor and an invitation to join a professional organization as inspiration for "More Distinction," a Saturday feature in the Buffalo Express *in June 1870. The zany, pun-filled story is reprinted, with commentary, and with three True Williams illustrations from the 1875* Sketches, New and Old *and two Tom Toles drawings from a 1978* Buffalo Courier-Express Sunday *magazine.*

Buffalo Express

JUNE 4, 1870

[FROM MARK TWAIN]
MORE DISTINCTION.

I have received the following notice:

THE WESTERN NEW YORK POULTRY SOCIETY,
BUFFALO, June 1, 1870.

MARK TWAIN, Esq.: Sir—At a recent meeting of the Executive Committee of the Western New York Poultry Society you were elected an honorary member of the Society.

E.C. DEANE,
Recording Secretary.

"It never rains but it pours." Neither do distinctions begin to fall upon a man in a sprinkle but very shortly they increase to a flood. Within the space of one short month I have been raised to the dignity of honorary membership in Agricultural, Horticultural and Vinicultural societies in the States of Iowa, Indiana, California, Massachusetts, Maryland and Pennsylvania, and now, as a culminating grandeur, I have become an honorary member of the Western New York Poultry Society, and my ravenous ambition is satisfied.

Seriously, from early youth I have taken an especial interest in the subject of poultry-raising, and so this membership touches a ready sympathy in my breast. Even as a school boy, poultry-raising was a study with me, and I may say without egotism that as early as the age of seventeen I was acquainted with all the best and speediest methods of raising chickens, from raising them off a roost by burning Lucifer matches under their noses, down to lifting them off a fence on a frosty night by insinuating the end of a warm board under their heels. By the time I was twenty years old, I really supposed I had raised more poultry than any one individual in all the section around there. The very chickens came to know my talent, by and by. The youth of both sexes ceased to paw the earth for worms, and the old roosters that came to crow "remained to pray," when I passed by.

I have had so much experience in the raising of fowls that I cannot but think that a few hints from me might be useful to the Society. The two methods I have already touched upon are very simple, and are only used in the raising of the commonest clans of fowls; one is for Summer, the other for Winter. In the one case, you start out with a friend along about eleven o'clock on a Summer's night, (not later, because in some States—especially California and Oregon—chickens always rouse up just at midnight and crow from ten to thirty minutes, according to the ease or difficulty they experience in getting the public waked up,) and your friend carries with him a sack. Arrived at the hen roost, (your neighbor's, not your own,) you light a match and hold it under first one and then another pullet's nose until they are willing to go into that bag without making any trouble about it. You then return home, either taking the bag with you or leaving it behind, according as circumstances shall dictate. N.B. I *have* seen the time when it was eligible and appropriate to leave the sack behind and walk off with considerable velocity, without ever leaving any word where to send it.

In the case of the other method mentioned for raising poultry, your friend takes along a covered vessel with a charcoal fire in it, and you carry a long slender plank. This is a frosty night, understand. Arrived at the tree or fence or other hen-roost, (your own, if you are an idiot,) you warm the end of your plank in your friend's fire vessel and then raise it aloft and ease it up gently against a slumbering chicken's feet. If the subject of your attentions is a true bird, he will infallibly return thanks with a sleepy cluck or two and step out and take up quarters on the plank, thus becoming so conspicuously accessory before the fact to his own murder as to make it a grave question in our minds, as it once was in the mind of Blackstone, whether he is not really and deliberately committing suicide in the second degree. [But you enter a contemplation of these legal refinements subsequently, not then.]

When you wish to raise a fine, donkey-voiced Shanghai rooster, you do it with a lasso, just as you would a bull. It is because he must be choked, and choked effectually, too. It is the only good, certain way, for whenever he mentions the matter which he is cordially interested in, the chances are ninety-nine in a hundred that he secures somebody else's immediate attention to it, too, whether it be day or night.

The Black Spanish is an exceedingly fine bird and a costly one. Thirty-five dollars is the usual figure, and fifty a not uncommon price for a specimen. Even its eggs are worth from a dollar to a dollar and a half apiece, and yet are so unwholesome that the city physician seldom orders them for the workhouse. Still I have once or twice procured as high as a dozen at a time for nothing, in the dark of the moon. The best way to raise the Black Spanish fowl, is to go late in the evening and raise coop and all. The reason I recommend this method, is, that the birds being so absurdly valuable, the owners do not permit them to roost around promiscuously, but put them in a coop as strong as a fire-proof safe, and keep it in the kitchen at night. The method I speak of is not always a bright and satisfying success, and yet there are so many little articles of *vertu* about a kitchen that if you fail on the coop you can generally bring away something else. I brought away a nice steel trap, one night, worth ninety cents.

But what is the use in my pouring out my whole intellect on this subject? I have shown the Western New York Poultry Society that they have taken to their bosom a party who is not a Spring chicken by any means, but a man who knows all about poultry, and is just as high up in the most efficient methods of raising it as the President of the institution himself. I thank these gentlemen right pleasantly and heartily for the honorary membership they have conferred upon me, and shall stand at all times ready and willing to testify my good feeling and my official zeal by deeds as well as by this hastily penned advice and information. Whenever they are ready to go to raising poultry, let them call for me just any evening after eleven o'clock and I shall be on hand promptly.

MARK TWAIN.

P.S.—To the Recording Secretary: I know two or three good places.

As Twain continued to work out of his home office well into 1870, another story idea easily within reach was partly inspired by his colorful neighbor, Mary Elizabeth Johnson Lord, who also lived on Delaware Street, less than two miles north of him.

Mary Lord, a beloved and legendary local character, was a generation older than Twain when they met. She was the daughter of Ebenezer Johnson, who became Buffalo's first mayor. Forty years earlier, she and John Lord had eloped and married. Reverend John Chase Lord became one of Buffalo's most influential clerics, presiding over Central Presbyterian Church for decades, and was known as the "Buffalo Thunderer" for his sermons. Twain admired Lord's private library of 10,260 books and pamphlets and joked about wanting to steal his rare volume of *Gentleman's Magazine and Historical Chronicle.*

Mary Lord often demonstrated her love of animals in eccentric ways. She would ride up and down Delaware Street in a miniature phaeton drawn by two, four, or six Shetland ponies, while her coachman tossed handfuls of birdseed for sparrows. She would sit in the middle of the street for hours reading the newspaper in order to ensure that wagon drivers were lightening loads for their horses, thus alienating teamsters. Lord also helped found Buffalo's Society for the Prevention of Cruelty to Animals.

The Lords' Gothic Revival home, named Oakwood, which Twain visited, occupied much of the city block on Delaware, near today's Potomac Avenue. Above the library fireplace was a stained-glass window based on a portrait of Mary beside her favorite dog, Grandfather Smallweed. Many of her other dogs, cats, and horses had unusual names like Caesar, Cleopatra, Peggoty Muggins, and Periwinkle. Children nibbled cookies while they petted and played with her menagerie of animals, which included livestock and chickens.

It was only natural, then, that when the newly formed Western New York Poultry Society awarded honorary membership to the *Buffalo Express* staff that Twain's creative imagination would comically connect the society with Mary Lord. The two were known to have discussed techniques for raising chickens.

The result was "More Distinction," a satirical and entertaining piece that appeared on page 2 of the *Express* on Saturday, June 4, 1870.

The seed for "More Distinction" was planted in a brief in late March about the creation of the Western New York Poultry Society, a local group of "poultry breeders and chicken fanciers." Their goal was to share information on "how to breed poultry, birds, and other animals" by means of reports and public fairs. Two months later, another *Express* brief announced that at a meeting the Poultry Society had made all members of the city press honorary members. Such proclamations seem to have been commonplace—in May, the board of trade also made the *Buffalo Express* staff honorary members.

Twain pounced on the possibilities of poultry punning.

He begins with a trademark gimmick fresh off the pages of *The Innocents Abroad*: setting up an amusing experience by stressing that he has longed to accomplish it since infancy or childhood. (See the Parisian barber episode in chapter 12, or the chapter 34 description of his Turkish bath in Constantinople.)

He follows with a series of pun permutations on multiple methods of "raising" (more like "hoisting and heisting") chickens. First, strike a match under a sleeping chicken's nose to startle it awake before plopping it in a sack. Or place a heated plank under the feet of an innocent chicken. Or simply lasso the desired chicken. Or, if all else fails, raise up the entire chicken coop and cart it away.

Twain closes with another pun on "spring chicken" and offers his continued expertise on late-night chicken thievery to his new Poultry Society comrades.

Ironically, in mid-February 1871, the *Express* published a long (full column and a half) story praising the Western New York Poultry Society's mammoth exhibition of hundreds of chickens, turkeys, geese, ducks, pigeons, doves, and a few rabbits in a well-attended five-day show. Only slightly tongue in cheek, the reporter crows with civic boosterism for a Buffalo known for its horseracing, industry, commerce, billiards, and now its claim as "cock of the walk."

But Twain, who had just returned from a business trip to Washington, DC, had his hands full at home with a seriously ill wife and infant son. He was likely unaware of the successful Poultry Society affair. In any event, he did not write a comic sequel to "More Distinction."

However, in 1875 Twain selected the story for inclusion in his *Sketches, New and Old* collection. Twain retitled it "To Raise Poultry" and approved three accompanying illustrations by True Williams. The first shows the Twain narrator and a nocturnal accomplice holding a warm plank under a chicken's heels to rouse it (figure 8.1); and Twain lighting a match under a chicken's beak while his co-conspirator waits with an open sack (figure 8.2); finally, Twain fleeing, not with an entire coop, but with only a stolen trap (figure 8.3).

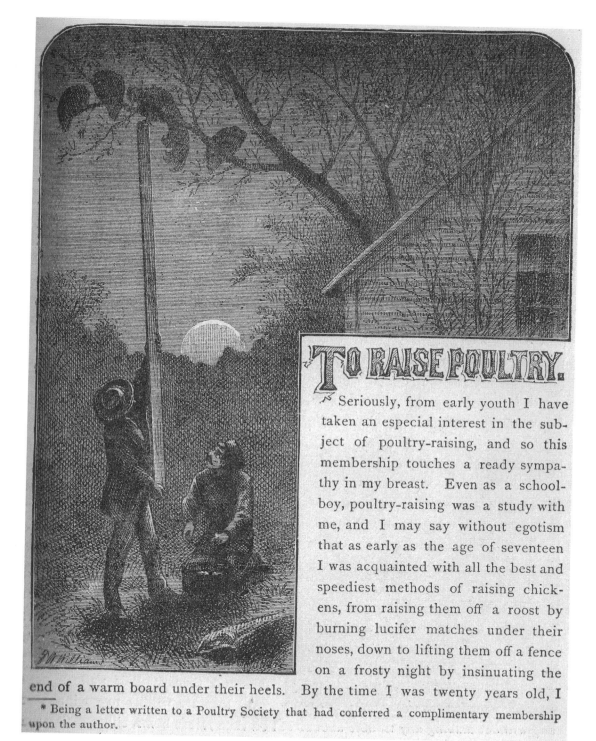

TO RAISE POULTRY.

Seriously, from early youth I have taken an especial interest in the subject of poultry-raising, and so this membership touches a ready sympathy in my breast. Even as a schoolboy, poultry-raising was a study with me, and I may say without egotism that as early as the age of seventeen I was acquainted with all the best and speediest methods of raising chickens, from raising them off a roost by burning lucifer matches under their noses, down to lifting them off a fence on a frosty night by insinuating the end of a warm board under their heels. By the time I was twenty years old, I

* Being a letter written to a Poultry Society that had conferred a complimentary membership upon the author.

FIGURE 8.1. Decorative chapter heading; illustration of men raising poultry with a warm plank by True Williams for Twain's *Buffalo Express* story "More Distinction." *Image from* Mark Twain's Sketches, New and Old *(Hartford, CT: American Publishing Company, 1875), 81*

FIGURE 8.2. Lighting a match under a chicken's nose; illustration by True Williams for Twain's *Buffalo Express* story "More Distinction." *Image from* Mark Twain's Sketches, New and Old *(Hartford, CT: American Publishing Company, 1875), 82*

FIGURE 8.3. Thief making away with a stolen trap; illustration by True Williams for Twain's *Buffalo Express* story "More Distinction." *Image from* Mark Twain's Sketches, New and Old *(Hartford, CT: American Publishing Company, 1875), 84*

More than one hundred years later, when "More Distinction" was reprinted in the *Buffalo Courier-Express Sunday* magazine, Tom Toles provided two of his own drawings, with the Twain narrator looking older, reflecting his mature mane of bushy white hair and wearing his customary white suit. Toles's first illustration depicts Twain struggling for leverage to raise a chicken with a warm plank (figure 8.4).

FIGURE 8.4. Twain narrator lifting warm plank under chicken's hindquarters; illustration by Tom Toles for Twain's *Buffalo Express* story "More Distinction." *Image from the* Buffalo Courier-Express Sunday *magazine, December 3, 1978. Courtesy of Buffalo State University Archives,* Courier-Express *Collection*

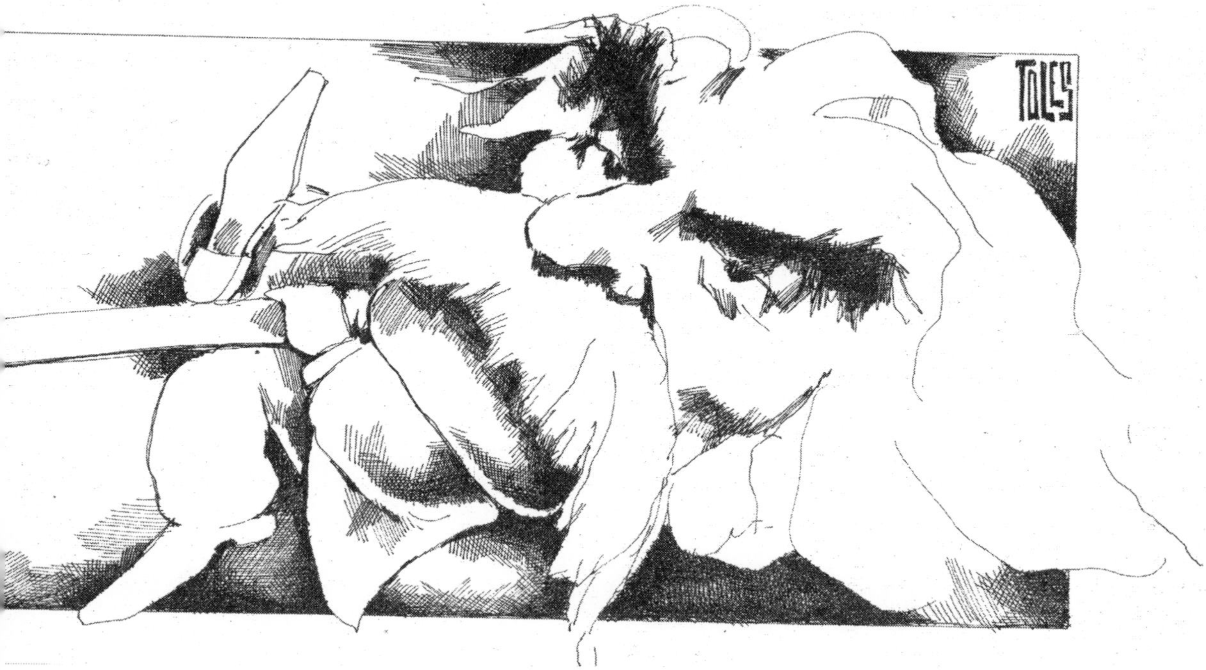
TOLES

The second Toles drawing shows Twain confidently lighting a match under a chicken's backside, with the distraught chicken flying up off its perch (figure 8.5).

FIGURE 8.5. Twain narrator lighting a match under chicken's posterior; illustration by Tom Toles for Twain's *Buffalo Express* story "More Distinction." *Image from the* Buffalo Courier-Express Sunday *magazine, December 3, 1978. Courtesy of Buffalo State University Archives,* Courier-Express *Collection*

CHAPTER NINE

WAR, WHAT IS IT GOOD FOR?

Absolutely Something, for Twain

*D*uring the late summer and into the fall of 1870, the national press and Buffalo Express *devoted lots of newspaper space to "non-news" about the impending, but very slowly developing, Franco-Prussian War. Twain had a field day with journalism's overreaction. In July he collaborated with John Hall, the composing foreman at the* Express, *to create hilarious blaring headlines to accompany a hoax war dispatch. Two months later, he published a masterly coup de grâce, combining his own skill as an illustrator with his biting writing wit. "The Fortifications of Paris," with Twain's farcical war map and equally funny text, became an instant international hit. He topped it off by writing a follow-up story in the* Express *about the sensation created by his satirical war map. The July, September, and October* Express *stories are reprinted here, with headlines designed by Twain and Twain's map of the fortifications of Paris, followed by commentary, and three clever illustrations by Tom Toles from a 1978 edition of the* Buffalo Courier-Express Sunday *magazine.*

Buffalo Express

JULY 25, 1870

THE EUROPEAN WAR!!!

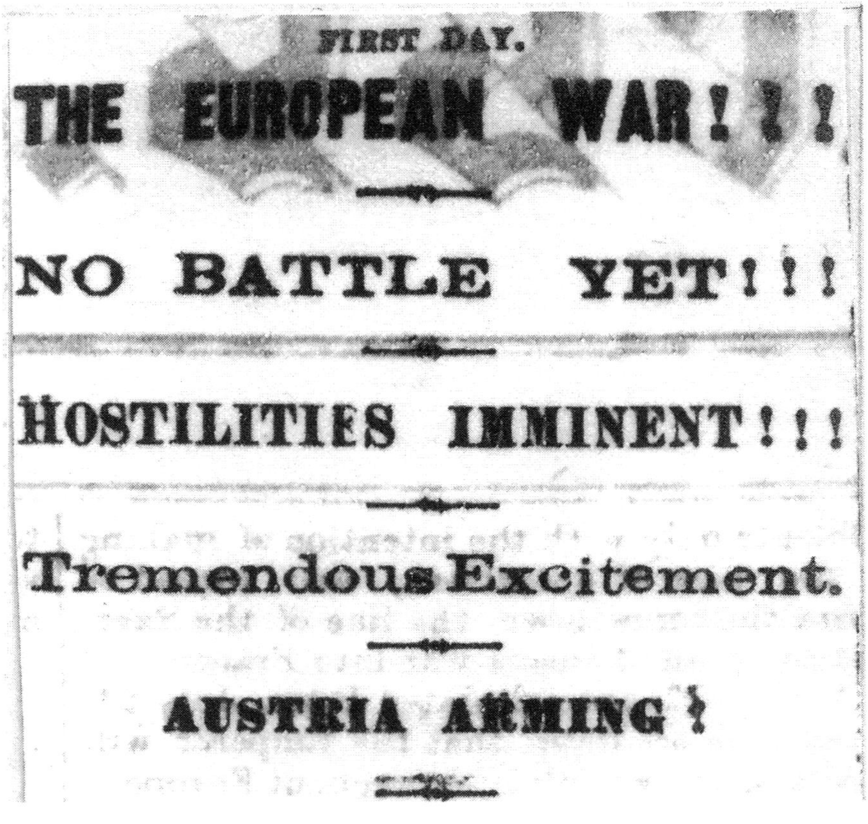
FIRST DAY.

THE EUROPEAN WAR!!!

NO BATTLE YET!!!

HOSTILITIES IMMINENT!!!

Tremendous Excitement.

AUSTRIA ARMING!

FIGURE 9.1. First Day: The European War. Mock headlines designed by Mark Twain to accompany his hoax war dispatch in the *Buffalo Express* datelined Berlin. *Image from the* Buffalo Express, *July 25, 1870*

Berlin, Tuesday.

No battle has been fought yet. But hostilities may burst forth any week.

There is tremendous excitement here over news from the front to the effect that two companies of French soldiers are assembling here.

It is rumored that Austria is arming—what with, is not known.

SECOND DAY.

THE EUROPEAN WAR,

NO BATTLE YET !

FIGHTING IMMINENT

AWFUL EXCITEMENT.

Russia Sides with Prussia !

ENGLAND NEUTRAL !

AUSTRIA NOT ARMING.

FIGURE 9.2. Second Day: The European War. Mock headlines designed by Mark Twain to accompany his phony *Buffalo Express* war dispatch story also "sent" from Berlin. *Image from the* Buffalo Express, *July 25, 1870*

Berlin, Wednesday.

No battle has been fought yet. However, all thoughtful men feel that the land may be drenched with blood before the Summer is over.

There is an awful excitement here over the rumor from the front that two companies of Prussian troops have concentrated on the border. German confidence remains unshaken!

There is news here to the effect that Russia espouses the cause of Prussia and will bring 4,000,000 men to the field.

England proclaims strict neutrality.

The report that Austria is arming needs confirmation.

THIRD DAY.

THE EUROPEAN WAR.

NO RATTLE YET!

BLOODSHED IMMINENT !

ENORMOUS EXCITEMENT ! ! !

INVASION OF PRUSSIA ! !

INVASION OF FRANCE !

Russia Sides With France ! ! !

England Still Neutral !

FIRING HEARD !

THE EMPEROR TO TAKE COMMAND.

FIGURE 9.3. Third Day: The European War. Mock headlines designed by Mark Twain to accompany his fake *Buffalo Express* war dispatch datelined Paris. *Image from the* Buffalo Express, *July 25, 1870*

No battle has been fought yet. But Field Marshal McMahon telegraphs thus to the Emperor:

"If the Frinch airmy survoives intil Christmas, there'll be throuble. Forninst this fact it wud be sagacious if the divil wint the rounds of his establishment to prepare for the occasion, and took the precaution to warrum up the Prussian department a bit agin the day. MIKE."

There is an enormous state of excitement here over news from the front to the effect that yesterday France and Prussia were simultaneously invaded by two bodies of troops which lately assembled on the border. Both armies conducted their invasions secretly, and are hunting around for each other on opposite sides of the line.

Russia espouses the cause of France. She will bring 200,000 men to the field.

England continues to remain neutral.

Firing was heard yesterday in the direction of Blucherburg, and for a while the excitement was intense. However, when the people reflected that the country in that direction is uninhabitable, and impassable by anything but birds, they became tranquil again.

The Emperor sends his troops to the field with immense enthusiasm. He will lead them in person, when they return.

FOURTH DAY.

THE EUROPEAN WAR!

NO BATTLE YET!

The Troops Growing Old!

But Bitter Strife Imminent!

PRODIGIOUS EXCITEMENT!

The Invasions Successfully Accomplished and the Invaders Safe!

Russia Sides with Both Sides.

ENGLAND WILL FIGHT BOTH!

FIGURE 9.4. Fourth Day: The European War. Mock headlines designed by Mark Twain to accompany his satirical *Buffalo Express* war dispatch supposedly sent from London. *Image from the* Buffalo Express, *July 25, 1870*

No battle has been fought, thus far, but a million impetuous soldiers are gritting their teeth at each other across the border, and the most serious fears are entertained that if they do not die of old age first, there will be bloodshed in this war yet.

The prodigious patriotic excitement goes on. In Prussia, per Prussian telegrams, though contradicted in France. In France, per French telegrams, though contradicted from Prussia.

The Prussian invasion of France was a magnificent success. The military failed to find the French, but made good their return to Prussia without the loss of a single man. The French invasion of Prussia is also demonstrated to have been a brilliant and successful achievement. The army failed to find the Prussians, but made good their return to the Vaterland without bloodshed, after having invaded as much as they wanted to.

There is glorious news from Russia to the effect that she will side with both sides.

Also from England—she will fight both sides.

London, Thursday evening.

I rushed over too soon. I shall return home in Tuesday's steamer and wait till the war begins.

MARK TWAIN.

𝔅𝔲𝔣𝔣𝔞𝔩𝔬 𝔈𝔵𝔭𝔯𝔢𝔰𝔰

SEPTEMBER 17, 1870

FORTIFICATIONS OF PARIS.

TO THE READER.

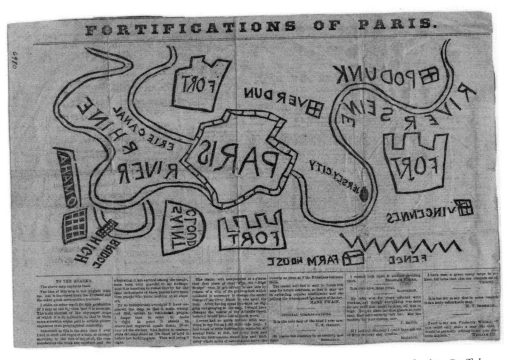

FIGURE 9.5. Fortifications of Paris war map; illustration by Mark Twain for his *Buffalo Express* story "Fortifications of Paris." *Image from the* Buffalo Express, *September 17, 1870. Courtesy of Buffalo State University Archives,* Courier-Express *Collection*

The above map explains itself.

The idea of this map is not original with me, but is borrowed from the *Tribune* and the other great metropolitan journals.

I claim no other merit for this production (if I may so call it,) than that it is accurate. The main blemish of the city-paper maps of which it is an imitation, is, that in them more attention seems paid to artistic picturesqueness than geographical reliability.

Inasmuch as this is the first time I ever tried to draft and engrave a map, or attempt anything in the line of art at all, the commendations the work has received and the admiration it has excited among the people, have been very grateful to my feelings. And it is touching to reflect that by far the most enthusiastic of these praises have come from people who know nothing at all about art.

By an unimportant oversight I have engraved the map so that it reads wrong-end first, except to left-handed people. I forgot that in order to make it right in print it should be drawn and engraved upside down. However let the student who desires to contemplate the map stand on his head or hold it before her looking-glass. That will bring it right.

The reader will comprehend at a glance that that piece of river with the "High Bridge" over it got left out to one side by reason of a slip of the graving-tool which rendered it necessary to change the entire course of the river Rhine or else spoil the map. After having spent two days in digging and gouging at the map, I would have changed the course of the Atlantic Ocean before I would have lost so much work.

I never had so much trouble with anything in my life as I did with this map. I had heaps of little fortifications scattered all around Paris, at first, but every now and then my instruments would slip and fetch away whole miles of batteries and leave the vicinity as clean as if the Prussians had been there.

The reader will find it well to frame this map for future reference, so that it may aid in extending popular intelligence and dispelling the wide-spread ignorance of the day.

MARK TWAIN.

OFFICIAL COMMENDATIONS.

It is the only map of the kind I ever saw.

U.S. GRANT.

It places the situation in an entirely new light.

BISMARCK.

I cannot look upon it without shedding tears.

BRIGHAM YOUNG.

It is very nice, large print.

NAPOLEON.

My wife was for years afflicted with freckles, and though everything was done for her relief that could be done, all was in vain. But, sir, since her first glance at your map, they have entirely left her. She has nothing but convulsions, now.

J. SMITH.

If I had had this map I could have got out of Metz without any trouble.

BAZAINE.

I have seen a great many maps in my time, but none that this one reminds me of.

TROCHU.

It is fair to say that in some respects it is a truly remarkable map.

W.T. SHERMAN.

I said to my son Frederick William, "If you could only make a map like that, I would be perfectly willing to see you die—even anxious."

WILLIAM III.

Buffalo Express

OCTOBER 15, 1870

MARK TWAIN.
HIS MAP OF THE FORTIFICATIONS OF PARIS

Mark Twain's map of the Fortifications of Paris is published in the *Galaxy* this month with the following explanatory introduction:

I published my "Map of the Fortifications of Paris" in my own paper a fortnight ago, but am obliged to reproduce it in the *Galaxy*, to satisfy the extraordinary demand for it which has arisen in military circles throughout the country. General Grant's outspoken commendation originated this demand, and General Sherman's fervent endorsement added fuel to it. The result is that tons of these maps have been fed to the suffering soldiers of our land, but without avail. They hunger still. We will cast the *Galaxy* into the breach and stand by and await the effect.

The next Atlantic mail will doubtless bring news of a European frenzy for the map. It is reasonable to expect that the siege of Paris will be suspended till a German translation of it can be forwarded (it is now in preparation), and that the defense of Paris will likewise be suspended to await the reception of the French translation (now progressing under my hands, and likely to be unique.) King William's high praise of the map and Napoleon's frank enthusiasm concerning its execution will ensure its prompt adoption in Europe as the only authoritative and legitimate exposition of the present military situation. It is plain that if the Prussians cannot get into Paris with the facilities afforded by this production of mine they ought to deliver the enterprise into abler hands.

Strangers to me keep insisting that this map does *not* "explain itself." One person came to me with bloodshot eyes and a harrassed look about him, and shook the map in my face and said he believed I was some new kind of idiot. I have been abused a good deal by other quick-tempered people like him, who came with similar complaints. Now, therefore, I yield willingly, and for the information of the ignorant will briefly explain the present military position as illustrated by the map. Part of the Prussian forces, under Prince Frederick William, are now boarding at the "farm-house" in the margin of the map. There is nothing between them and Vincennes but a rail fence in bad repair. Any corporal can see at a glance that they have only to burn it, pull it down, crawl under, climb over, or walk around it, just as the commander-in-chief shall elect.

Another portion of the Prussian forces are at Podunk, under Von Moltke. They have nothing to do but to float down the Seine on a raft and scale the walls of Paris. Let the worshippers of that overrated soldier believe in him still, and abide the result—for me, *I* do not believe he will even think of a raft. At Omaha and the High Bridge are vast masses of Prussian infantry, and it is only fair to say that they are likely to *stay* there, as that figure of a window-sash between them stands for a brewery. Away up out of sight over the top of the map is the fleet of the Prussian navy, ready at any moment to come cavorting down the Erie Canal (unless some new iniquity of an unprincipled Legislature shall put up the tolls and so render it cheaper to walk.) To me it looks as if Paris is a singularly close place. She was never situated before as she is in this map.

MARK TWAIN.

URING THE SUMMER AND FALL OF 1870, TWAIN'S DOMESTIC SCENE was in turmoil. He and his wife frequently shuttled back and forth by train between Buffalo and Elmira to be at the bedside of his dying father-in-law and benefactor, Jervis Langdon. After Langdon died in August, a girlfriend of Olivia's from Elmira stayed with Olivia in her Buffalo home to help comfort her in her grief, but her friend contracted typhoid fever and died in the master bedroom in September. Furthermore, Olivia experienced a difficult final trimester of pregnancy, resulting in a near miscarriage in October and the premature birth of a son in November, a child who would die before his second year.

Throughout this tremendous emotional strife, Twain found the wherewithal to write a comic series of stories satirizing the Franco-Prussian War. Looking back at that time, thirty-five years later, Twain commented on this strangely creative interlude: "The resulting periodical and sudden changes of mood in me, from deep melancholy to half insane tempests and cyclones of humor, are among the curiosities of my life."[1]

Although Twain's satirical map, "Fortifications of Paris," was published in the September 17, 1870, *Buffalo Express*, his "spasm of humorous possession" related to the Franco-Prussian War actually began in July.

As rumors rumbled about the conflict between France and Germany in the summer of 1870, Twain was amused by the sensationalized page 1 banner headlines, with their dire forecasts of the impending battle in bold-faced type, wildly punctuated by exclamation points. The hyped-up drumbeat of reportage from the European field appeared steadily from July through September in major US newspapers and in his own *Buffalo Express*.

Twain had patiently read a week's worth of center front-page *Express* accounts of the growing strife in Europe, always under an exaggerated WAR NEWS banner. *New York Tribune* telegraphic reports of war activity—or, rather, non-activity—accompanied by several hysterical subheads suggesting nations taking sides (ITALY TO ASSIST FRANCE), frequently concluded with no news at all (NO BATTLE YET; NO FORMAL PROCLAMATION YET ISSUED).

But the Saturday, July 23 *Express* page 1 treatment of the war, with its vertical series of nine stacked headlines and field stories datelined Madrid, London, and Paris, took the cake, igniting Twain's satirical muse.

In the following Monday edition (there was no Sunday edition), Twain parodied the *Express*'s hyperbolic coverage on page 2 by perpetuating one of his patented literary hoaxes, complete with his fake byline as European war correspondent. His entry occupied an entire column and purported to cover war progress over a four-day stretch (figures 9.1, 9.2, 9.3, 9.4).

Twain's close relationship with his *Express* composing room foreman was apparent in his preposterously fabricated headlines, appearing to come from Berlin, Paris, and London, peppered with exclamation points to achieve optimum ridicule.

With his phony headlines and "stories" from the field, Twain effectively shredded the war misinformation being spread by real war reporters trying to scoop each other with shifting national allegiances and inconsequential military skirmishes but no credible sources. Twain's "dispatches" all blare NO BATTLE YET!

Two months later, perhaps drawing from one of the real *Express* headlines of July 25 (PARIS BEING FORTIFIED),[2] Twain used his knowledge of newspaper printing to create a satirical battlefront map—"Fortifications of Paris"—depicting French military plans to guard Paris from the impending Prussian army assault (figure 9.5).

As Twain recalled, "I sent down to my newspaper office for a huge wooden capital *M* and turned it upside-down, and carved a crude and absurd map of Paris upon it, and published it, along with a sufficiently absurd description of it, with guarded and imaginary compliments of it bearing the signatures of General Grant and other experts."[3]

But at least two of his *Express* colleagues remembered him sitting at his newspaper desk for either half a day or for two days, whittling the map with a jackknife onto a wooden block, chuckling as he did so. Twain was well aware that the lettering in the drawing would appear in print backward. It is said that when the presses ran in the basement shortly after midnight on September 17, Twain "in person supervised the taking of the proofs."[4]

Twain picked Saturday, September 17, to publish the map with humorous commentary, because the Saturday *Buffalo Express* always sold the most copies. The map was prominently displayed across six columns at the top of page 2. Sure enough, the edition quickly sold out. So the "Fortifications of Paris" map was reprinted the next Wednesday morning in the *Weekly Express* as a 14½-by-11-inch broadside insert. It was also published in the November issue of the *Galaxy* as "Mark Twain's Map of Paris."

Because of newspaper exchange agreements, Twain's amusing Paris map quickly attracted national and global attention. Shortly after the map appeared, the *Cleveland Herald* printed a blurb about successfully duplicating Twain's supposedly "uncopyable" map[5] by sprinkling corn feed on a printing block and allowing chickens with tar on their feet to scratch all over it. No stranger to self-promotion, Twain himself exploited the widespread interest with a follow-up story in the October 15 *Express*.

Twain claimed in later years that the map was circulated in Berlin beer halls and entertained American students, while confusing German soldiers.

His extended riff on absurd elements of the Franco-Prussian War ended with a bizarre parting *Express* story in mid-December, "War and 'Whittles,'" an imaginative fantasy about blockaded Parisian residents of various social classes raiding the city zoo for food.

His masterly literary hoax enabled Twain to showcase his career-long running gag of poking fun at the French. And as a Buffalonian, he quite conveniently sided with the Germans in the conflict. By 1855, 39 percent of the heads of households in Buffalo were from German states. *Express* help-wanted ads sought "German or American" or "German preferred" girls to cook or do housework. Twain even named one of the cats in his Buffalo home "Fraulein."

When Twain's September 17 Paris map and October 15 follow-up story were reprised one hundred years later in the *Buffalo Courier-Express Sunday* magazine by reporter Michael Hiltzik, staff illustrator Tom Toles supplied three witty drawings of reactions to the map via caricatures of Grant (figure 9.6), Bismarck (figure 9.7), and Napoleon III (figure 9.8).

Toles's depiction of Bismarck adds an original comic touch by interpreting the "official commendation" attributed to him by Twain (in the October 15 story) as Bismarck lighting the rolled-up Paris map to stoke a cigar!

GRANT : "ONE OF A KIND."

FIGURE 9.6. Grant: "One of a Kind"; illustration by Tom Toles for Twain's *Buffalo Express* story "Fortifications of Paris." *Image from the* Buffalo Courier-Express Sunday *magazine, July 2, 1978. Courtesy of Buffalo State University Archives,* Courier-Express *Collection*

BISMARCK : "AN ENTIRELY NEW LIGHT."

FIGURE 9.7. Bismarck: "An Entirely New Light"; illustration by Tom Toles for Twain's *Buffalo Express* story "Fortifications of Paris." *Image from the* Buffalo Courier-Express Sunday *magazine, July 2, 1978. Courtesy of Buffalo State University Archives,* Courier-Express Collection

NAPOLEON III : "NICE LARGE PRINT."

FIGURE 9.8. Napoleon III: "Nice Large Print"; illustration by Tom Toles for Twain's *Buffalo Express* story "Fortifications of Paris." *Image from the* Buffalo Courier-Express Sunday *magazine, July 2, 1978. Courtesy of Buffalo State University Archives,* Courier-Express Collection

NOTES

INTRODUCTION

1. Walter Blair, *Native American Humor* (New York: HarperCollins, 1960).

2. Beverly R. David, *Mark Twain and His Illustrators 1869–1875* (Troy, NY: Whitson, 1986).

3. Earl D. Berry, "Mark Twain as a Newspaper Man," *Buffalo Express*, November 11, 1917, 40.

4. Samuel L. Clemens to Mary Mason Fairbanks, September 26 and 27, 1869, in *Mark Twain's Letters*, ed. Victor Fischer and Michael B. Frank, vol. 3, *1869* (Berkeley: University of California Press, 1992), 368.

5. John Harrison Mills, "Memories of a Buffalo Artist," *Buffalo Express*, November 5, 1916.

6. John Harrison Mills, "When Mark Twain Lived in Buffalo: Reminiscent Aspects of the Humorist's Life in This City, as Recollected by One Whose Work Brought Him into Close and Daily Association with Him," *Buffalo Sunday Morning News*, May 15, 1910.

7. Thomas J. Reigstad, "John Harrison Mills: Twain's Unsung *Buffalo Express* Illustrator," *Mark Twain Journal* 56, no. 1 (Spring 2018): 86–101.

8. "Mark Twain Is on the Road to Last Long Slumber," *Buffalo Illustrated Sunday Times*, April 24, 1910, 46.

9. Barbara Schmidt, "The Life and Art of True Williams," *Mark Twain Journal* 39, no. 2 (Fall 2001): 1–60.

10. Albert Bigelow Paine, *Mark Twain: A Biography* (New York: Harper & Brothers, 1912), 366.

11. Samuel L. Clemens to William Dean Howells, January 18, 1876, in *The Selected Letters of Mark Twain*, ed. Charles Neider (New York: Harper & Row, 1982), 88.

12. Samuel L. Clemens to Olivia Langdon, March 6, 1869, in *Mark Twain's Letters*, 3:138.

13. Schmidt, "The Life and Art," 6.

14. The *Sunday* magazine series included these reprinted Twain stories, Hiltzik introductions, and new Toles illustrations: "Mark Twain: The Fortifications of Paris," July 2, 1978, 12–14, 15, and 17 (with three Toles drawings); "A Mysterious Visit," July 7, 1978,

9–12 (with two Toles illustrations); "The Last Words of Great Men," October 8, 1978, 6–7, 9 (with four Toles illustrations); and "More Distinction," December 3, 1978, 16–17, 19 (with two Toles illustrations).

15. Michael A. Hiltzik, email to author, July 16, 2021.

16. "Mark Twain in Cartoon," *Mark Twain Journal* 49, no. 1/2 (Spring/Fall 2011): 67–72.

17. Thomas A. Tenney, "Calvin and Hobbes," *Mark Twain Journal* 23, no. 2 (Fall 1985): 1.

18. Jeff Simon, "At Long Last, a Definitive Look at Mark Twain's Buffalo Years," *Buffalo News*, February 24, 2013, F9.

19. Thomas J. Reigstad, "Making the Case That *Huck Finn* Is More about Children Than Race," *Buffalo News*, December 28, 2014, C5. This Zyglis illustration was published a second time, to accompany another book review, as well: Thomas J. Reigstad, "Twain vs. the World in Final Volume of Complete *Autobiography*," *Buffalo News*, September 20, 2015, D5.

CHAPTER ONE

1. In its review of Twain's retelling of Adam and Eve at the Falls, his former newspaper, the *Illustrated Buffalo Express*, panned the story as "a specimen of the author's feeblest humor and worst taste." "It has some very funny touches, but as a whole we don't like it," the paper wrote. "Of Special Local Interest," *Illustrated Buffalo Express*, June 25, 1893. Edward W. Bok of the *Buffalo Courier* was kinder, calling it "a humorous article." "Literary Letter," *Buffalo Courier*, June 18, 1893.

2. Paul Fatout, ed. *Mark Twain Speaking* (Iowa City: University of Iowa Press, 1976), 547.

CHAPTER TWO

1. Samuel L. Clemens to Mary Mason Fairbanks, September 27, 1869, in *Mark Twain to Mrs. Fairbanks*, ed. Dixon Wecter (San Marino, CA: Huntington Library, 1949), 109.

2. Mark Twain, "Arthur," *Buffalo Courier-Express Sunday* magazine, August 22, 1982, 10–11.

3. Joseph B. McCullough and Janice McIntire-Strasburg, eds. *Mark Twain at the Buffalo Express* (DeKalb: Northern Illinois Press, 1999).

4. Adam Zyglis, email messages to the author, January 31 and February 2, 2023.

CHAPTER FOUR

1. Samuel L. Clemens to Olivia Langdon Clemens, September 7, 1869, *Mark Twain's Letters*, ed. Victor Fischer and Michael B. Frank, vol. 3, *1869* (Berkeley: University of California Press, 1992), 345.

2. Samuel L. Clemens to Mary Mason Fairbanks, September 27, 1869, *Mark Twain to Mrs. Fairbanks*, ed. Dixon Wecter (San Marino, CA: Huntington Library Publications, 1949), 106.

3. Ron Powers, *Mark Twain: A Life* (New York: Simon & Schuster, 2005), 627.

CHAPTER FIVE

1. Harriet Beecher Stowe, "The True Story of Lady Byron's Life," *Atlantic Monthly*, September, 1869, 295–313.

2. For example, Twain attacks lovers of gossip and sensation in a September 2, 1869, "People and Things": "Byron collars are in vogue again"; in the next day's column he sarcastically observes that Stowe's article drove scads of readers with sordid appetites to buy Byron's works: "It is estimated that more copies of Lord Byron's works have been sold in this country within the last fifteen days than in seven years previously. And what is particularly aggravating, is, that people *read* the book now, whereas they used only to buy it for Christmas presents and centre-table ornaments"; and in his September 14 column, he playfully twists the truth with: "One DeLuna Byron, who was on Fremont's staff in Missouri, claims to be a legitimate son of Byron, and that his mother, a Spanish woman, being the first wife of the poet, Lady B., must have been an illegal wife."

CHAPTER SIX

1. Lucian C. Warren, "Mark Twain's Tale on Taxes Still Has Some Bite," *Buffalo Courier-Express*, January 12, 1961. Twain himself liked the story so much that he included it in his 1875 collection, *Sketches, New and Old*, although he changed the name of the *Buffalo Express* to the *Daily Warhoop*. He also appreciated the positive feedback he received on the story from his trusted reader in Cleveland, Mary "Mother" Fairbanks, writing on March 22, 1870: "Mother dear, I am glad you liked the Revenue article" (Dixon Wecter, ed., *Mark Twain to Mrs. Fairbanks* [San Marino, CA: Huntington Library Publications, 1949], 127).

CHAPTER SEVEN

1. Glenn R. P. Atwell, "The Delaware & North Street Cemetery," *Western New York Genealogical Society Journal* 38, no. 1 (June 2011).

CHAPTER NINE

1. Mark Twain, *Autobiography of Mark Twain*, vol. 1, ed. Harriet Elinor Smith (Berkeley: University of California Press, 2010), 362.

2. The Monday, July 25 *Express* came close to the previous cake-taking Saturday edition with an entire column trumpeting THE WAR news: eight stacked headlines (including A SLIGHT SKIRMISH; PARIS BEING FORTIFIED; HUNGARY FOR FRANCE; and DENMARK DECIDED ON WAR) and on-the-ground reports from Strasbourg, Paris, Marseilles, Berlin, Brussels, and two from New York City.

3. Twain, *Autobiography of Mark Twain*, 362.

4. "Two Excessively Rare Clemens Items," *First Editions and Autograph Letters* and *Manuscripts by Famous American Authors* (New York: American Art Association Anderson Galleries, 1936), 22.

5. "Mark Twain's Map," *Buffalo Express*, September 24, 1870.